I0455177

Greatest Hits of ...

THE 1950's

A Cross-Reference Manual

Greatest Hits of ...

THE 1950'S

A CROSS-REFERENCE MANUAL

Albert L. Kelley

ABSOLUTELY AMAZING eBOOKS

Absolutely Amazing eBooks

Published by Whiz Bang LLC, 926 Truman Avenue, Key West, Florida 33040, USA

Greatest Hits of ... The 1950's copyright © 2014 by Albert L. Kelley. Electronic compilation/ print edition copyright © 2014 by Whiz Bang LLC.

All rights reserved. No part of this book may be reproduced, scanned, or transmitted in any form or by any means, electronic or mechanical, including photocopying, recording, or any information storage and retrieval system, without permission in writing from the publisher. Please do not participate in or encourage piracy of copyrighted materials in violation of the author's rights. Purchase only authorized ebook editions.

Any names used herein are either not of an actual person or company, or if an actual person or company, used solely as an example. While the author has made every effort to provide accurate information at the time of publication, neither the publisher nor the author assumes any responsibility for errors, or for changes that occur after publication. Further, the publisher does not have any control over and does not assume any responsibility for author or third-party websites or their contents.

For information contact:
Publisher@AbsolutelyAmazingEbooks.com

ISBN-13: 978-1503303911
ISBN-10: 1503303918

DEDICATION

I want to thank my family for giving me such a broad based exposure to music. My Father introduced me to folk, my Mother to vocalists, my Sister to pop, my Brother to rock and my Aunt to a lot in between. Also to my oldest friend Dave Williams who introduced me to the eclectic tastes of the shock rock of Alice Cooper and the country music of Willie Nelson. And to everyone else who has ever introduced me to any new Artist, I thank you all. Finally to my wife for her support and editorial help. I love you.

TABLE OF CONTENTS

INTRODUCTION

The 1950's brought a wealth of music that still remains popular on the radio today. It was a transitional period from the orchestral hits of Guy Lombardo and the vocal stylings of Frank Sinatra and Perry Como to the folk music of the Weavers to the early rock of Bill Haley and the Comets, Jerry Lee Lewis and Little Richard. It was a time of the American songbook tunes like Doggie In The Window and Doo Wop songs like Why Do Fools Fall In Love. It was the decade that saw the end of the life and career of Mario Lanza. And it was the start of the career of a young singer named Elvis Presley. It was the decade that laid the foundations of all music that was to follow.

This book is not a history of music, but a reference manual. It lists the top 100 songs for each year in the 1950's (From 1950-1955, only the top 30 songs were tracked, so rather than reviewing 1,000 songs, the book only covers 580 songs). Then I have cross-referenced those songs by song title, men, women, groups, one-hit wonders and repeaters. While I had considered also categorizing the songs by genre, that classification is too vague. What is folk music to some is easy listening to others. As such, I only based the categories on verifiable areas.

The Master Song List is taken from Billboard Magazine's Top 100 list. While top performance lists had existed as early as the 1940's (often limited to a particular town or region), it wasn't standardized until the 1950's. The chart continued to evolve until Billboard created the first Top 100 chart in 1955. In 1958, the list was retitled The Hot 100. Billboard's other rankings, including Most Played in Jukeboxes and Most Played By Jockeys, had been discontinued by 1958 in favor of this single listing. The Hot 100 is now considered the primary listing of the most popular songs in America. It is ranked by radio airplay, audience impressions, sales data and streaming activities.

I have tried to be as faithful as possible to the listings. In some cases information was modified to clarify or correct an error.

THE MASTER LIST

		1950	
1950	1	Gordon Jenkins and The Weavers	Goodnight Irene
1950	2	Nat King Cole	Mona Lisa
1950	3	Anton Karas	Third Man Theme
1950	4	Gary and Bing Crosby	Sam's Song
1950	5	Gary and Bing Crosby	Simple Melody
1950	6	Teresa Brewer	Music, Music, Music
1950	7	Guy Lombardo	Third Man Theme
1950	8	Red Foley	Chattanoogie Shoe Shine Boy
1950	9	Sammy Kaye	Harbor Lights
1950	10	Sammy Kaye and Don Cornell	It Isn't Fair
1950	11	Eileen Barton	If I Knew You Were Coming I'd've Baked A Cake
1950	12	Kay Starr	Bonaparte's Retreat
1950	13	Gordon Jenkins and The Weavers	Tzena, Tzena, Tzena
1950	14	Tony Martin	There's No Tomorrow
1950	15	Phil Harris	The Thing
1950	16	Ames Brothers	Sentimental Me
1950	17	Andrews Sisters and Gordon Jenkins	I Wanna Be Loved
1950	18	Patti Page	Tennessee Waltz

1950	19	Andrews Sisters and Gordon Jenkins	I Can Dream, Can't I
1950	20	Tennessee Ernie Ford and Kay Starr	I'll Never Be Free
1950	21	Patti Page	All My Love
1950	22	Gordon Jenkins	My Foolish Heart
1950	23	Ames Brothers	Rag Mop
1950	24	Bill Snyder	Bewitched
1950	25	Perry Como	Hoop-Dee-Doo
1950	26	Gordon Jenkins	Bewitched
1950	27	Ames Brothers	Can Anyone Explain?
1950	28	Billy Eckstine	My Foolish Heart
1950	29	Bing Crosby	Dear Hearts And Gentle People
1950	30	Frankie Laine	Cry Of The Wild Goose
		1951	
1951	1	Nat King Cole	Too Young
1951	2	Tony Bennett	Because Of You
1951	3	Les Paul and Mary Ford	How High The Moon
1951	4	Rosemary Clooney	Come On-a My House
1951	5	Mario Lanza	Be My Love
1951	6	Weavers	On Top Of Old Smoky
1951	7	Tony Bennett	Cold, Cold Heart
1951	8	Perry Como	If
1951	9	Mario Lanza	Loveliest Night Of The Year
1951	10	Patti Page	Tennessee Waltz
1951	11	Frankie Laine	Jezebel
1951	12	Tony Martin	I Get Ideas
1951	13	Les Paul and Mary Ford	Mockin' Bird Hill
1951	14	Patti Page	Mockin' Bird Hill

1951	15	Guy Mitchell and Mitch Miller	My Heart Cries For You
1951	16	Eddy Howard	(It's No) Sin
1951	17	Vaughn Monroe	Sound Off
1951	18	Dinah Shore	Sweet Violets
1951	19	Les Paul and Mary Ford	The World Is Waiting For The Sunrise
1951	20	Guy Mitchell and Mitch Miller	My Truly, Truly Fair
1951	21	Four Aces and Al Alberts	(It's No) Sin
1951	22	Debbie Reynolds and Carleton Carpenter	Aba Daba Honeymoon
1951	23	Frankie Laine	Rose, Rose I Love You
1951	24	Del Wood	Down Yonder
1951	25	Billy Eckstine	I Apologize
1951	26	Patti Page	Would I Love You
1951	27	Perry Como and The Fontane Sisters	You're Just In Love
1951	28	Ames Brothers and Les Brown	Undecided
1951	29	Phil Harris	The Thing
1951	30	Les Baxter	Because Of You
		1952	
1952	1	Leroy Anderson	Blue Tango
1952	2	Kay Starr	Wheel Of Fortune
1952	3	Johnnie Ray	Cry
1952	4	Jo Stafford	You Belong To Me
1952	5	Vera Lynn	Auf Wiederseh'n, Sweetheart
1952	6	Rosemary Clooney	Half As Much

1952	7	Eddie Fisher and Hugo Winterhalter	Wish You Were Here
1952	8	Patti Page	I Went To Your Wedding
1952	9	Al Martino	Here In My Heart
1952	10	Percy Faith	Delicado
1952	11	Georgia Gibbs	Kiss Of Fire
1952	12	Eddie Fisher and Hugo Winterhalter	Anytime
1952	13	Four Aces	Tell Me Why
1952	14	Ella Mae Morse	Blacksmith Blues
1952	15	Jo Stafford	Jambalaya
1952	16	Rosemary Clooney	Botch-a-me
1952	17	Doris Day	A Guy Is A Guy
1952	18	Johnnie Ray	The Little White Cloud That Cried
1952	19	Frankie Laine	High Noon
1952	20	Eddie Fisher and Hugo Winterhalter	I'm Yours
1952	21	Mills Brothers	Glow Worm
1952	22	Johnny Standley	It's In The Book
1952	23	Pee Wee King	Slow Poke
1952	24	Johnnie Ray	Walkin' My Baby Back Home
1952	25	Les Paul	Meet Mr. Callaghan
1952	26	Don Cornell	I'm Yours
1952	27	Don Cornell	I'll Walk Alone
1952	28	Eddie Fisher and Hugo Winterhalter	Tell Me Why
1952	29	Hilltoppers	Trying
1952	30	Johnnie Ray	Please, Mr. Sun

		1953	
1953	1	Percy Faith	Song From Moulin Rouge
1953	2	Les Paul and Mary Ford	Vaya Con Dios
1953	3	Patti Page	Doggie In The Window
1953	4	Eddie Fisher	I'm Walking Behind You
1953	5	Ames Brothers	You, You, You
1953	6	Teresa Brewer	Till I Waltz Again With You
1953	7	Les Baxter	April In Portugal
1953	8	Perry Como	No Other Love
1953	9	Perry Como	Don't Let The Stars Get In Your Eyes
1953	10	Frankie Laine	I Believe
1953	11	Pee Wee Hunt	Oh
1953	12	Frank Chacksfield	Ebb Tide
1953	13	Nat King Cole	Pretend
1953	14	Richard Hayman	Ruby
1953	15	Stan Freberg	St. George And The Dragonet
1953	16	Hilltoppers	P.S. I Love You
1953	17	Gaylords	Tell Me You're Mine
1953	18	Julius La Rosa	Eh Cumpari
1953	19	Tony Bennett	Rags To Riches
1953	20	Silvana Mangano	Anna
1953	21	Perry Como	Say You're Mine Again
1953	22	Ray Anthony	Dragnet
1953	23	Frankie Laine and Jimmy Boyd	Tell Me A Story
1953	24	June Valli	Crying In The Chapel
1953	25	Joni James	Why Don't You Believe Me
1953	26	Joni James	Your Cheating Heart

1953	27	Frank Chacksfield	Limelight (Terry's Theme)
1953	28	Eddie Fisher	With These Hands
1953	29	Eartha Kitt	C'est Si Bon
1953	30	Joni James	Have You Heard?
		1954	
1954	1	Kitty Kallen	Little Things Mean A Lot
1954	2	Perry Como	Wanted
1954	3	Rosemary Clooney	Hey There
1954	4	Crew Cuts	Sh-Boom
1954	5	Jo Stafford	Make Love To Me
1954	6	Eddie Fisher	Oh! My Pa-pa
1954	7	Four Knights	I Get So Lonely
1954	8	Four Aces	Three Coins In The Fountain
1954	9	Doris Day	Secret Love
1954	10	Archie Bleyer	Hernando's Hideaway
1954	11	Frank Sinatra	Young At Heart
1954	12	Rosemary Clooney	This Ole House
1954	13	Eddie Fisher	I Need You Now
1954	14	Patti Page	Cross Over The Bridge
1954	15	Gaylords	The Little Shoemaker
1954	16	Dean Martin	That's Amore
1954	17	Frank Weir	The Happy Wanderer
1954	18	Nat King Cole	Answer Me My Love
1954	19	Tony Bennett	Stranger In Paradise
1954	20	Doris Day	If I Give My Heart To You
1954	21	Kay Starr	If You Love Me (Really Love Me)
1954	22	Ralph Marterie	Skokiaan
1954	23	Don Cornell	Hold My Hand
1954	24	Patti Page	Changing Partners

1954	25	Perry Como	Papa Loves Mambo
1954	26	Bill Haley and His Comets	Shake, Rattle And Roll
1954	27	Tony Bennett	Rags To Riches
1954	28	Kitty Kallen	In The Chapel In The Moonlight
1954	29	Four Aces	Stranger In Paradise
1954	30	Tony Martin	Here
		1955	
1955	1	Perez Prado	Cherry Pink And Apple Blossom White
1955	2	Bill Haley and His Comets	Rock Around The Clock
1955	3	Mitch Miller	The Yellow Rose Of Texas
1955	4	Roger Williams	Autumn Leaves
1955	5	Les Baxter	Unchained Melody
1955	6	Bill Hayes	The Ballad Of Davy Crockett
1955	7	Four Aces	Love Is A Many Splendored Thing
1955	8	McGuire Sisters	Sincerely
1955	9	Pat Boone	Ain't That A Shame
1955	10	Georgia Gibbs	Dance With Me Henry
1955	11	Crazy Otto	Crazy Otto Medley I and II
1955	12	Billy Vaughn	Melody Of Love
1955	13	Tennessee Ernie Ford	Sixteen Tons
1955	14	Frank Sinatra	Learnin' The Blues
1955	15	Fontaine Sisters	Hearts Of Stone
1955	16	Georgia Gibbs	Tweedle Dee
1955	17	Four Lads	Moments To Remember
1955	18	Chordettes	Mr. Sandman
1955	19	Joan Weber	Let Me Go Lover
1955	20	Nat King Cole	A Blossom Fell

1955	21	Al Hibbler	Unchained Melody
1955	22	Fess Parker	The Ballad Of Davy Crockett
1955	23	Art Mooney	Honey Babe
1955	24	Tennessee Ernie Ford	The Ballad Of Davy Crockett
1955	25	Perry Como	Ko Ko Mo
1955	26	Gisele Mackenzie	Hard To Get
1955	27	Ames Brothers	The Naughty Lady Of Shady Lane
1955	28	Jaye P. Morgan	That's All I Want From You
1955	29	Platters	Only You
1955	30	Somethin' Smith and The Redheads	It's A Sin To Tell A Lie
		1956	
1956	1	Elvis Presley	Heartbreak Hotel
1956	2	Elvis Presley	Don't Be Cruel
1956	3	Nelson Riddle	Lisbon Antigua
1956	4	Platters	My Prayer
1956	5	Gogi Grant	The Wayward Wind
1956	6	Les Baxter	The Poor People Of Paris
1956	7	Doris Day	Whatever Will Be Will Be (Que Sera Sera)
1956	8	Elvis Presley	Hound Dog
1956	9	Dean Martin	Memories Are Made Of This
1956	10	Kay Starr	Rock And Roll Waltz
1956	11	Morris Stoloff	Moonglow And Theme From "Picnic"
1956	12	Platters	The Great Pretender
1956	13	Pat Boone	I Almost Lost My Mind
1956	14	Elvis Presley	I Want You, I Need You, I Love You

1956	15	Elvis Presley	Love Me Tender
1956	16	Perry Como	Hot Diggity
1956	17	Eddie Heywood and Hugo Winterhalter	Canadian Sunset
1956	18	Carl Perkins	Blue Suede Shoes
1956	19	Jim Lowe	The Green Door
1956	20	Four Lads	No, Not Much
1956	21	Bill Doggett	Honky Tonk
1956	22	Tennessee Ernie Ford	Sixteen Tons
1956	23	Johnnie Ray	Just Walking In The Rain
1956	24	Patti Page	Allegheny Moon
1956	25	Fats Domino	I'm In Love Again
1956	26	Patience and Prudence	Tonight You Belong To Me
1956	27	Gene Vincent	Be-Bop-A-Lula
1956	28	Frankie Lymon and The Teenagers	Why Do Fools Fall In Love
1956	29	Four Lads	Standing On The Corner
1956	30	Buchanan and Goodman	The Flying Saucer
1956	31	George Cates	Moonglow And Theme From Picnic
1956	32	Cathy Carr	Ivory Tower
1956	33	Bill Haley and His Comets	See You Later Alligator
1956	34	Pat Boone	I'll Be Home
1956	35	Vic Damone	On The Street Where You Live
1956	36	Platters	Magic Touch
1956	37	Chordettes	Born To Be With You
1956	38	Don Cherry	Band Of Gold
1956	39	Perry Como	More
1956	40	Guy Mitchell	Singing The Blues

1956	41	Fats Domino	Blueberry Hill
1956	42	Sanford Clark	The Fool
1956	43	Don Robertson	The Happy Whistler
1956	44	Bing Crosby and **Grace Kelly**	True Love
1956	45	Little Richard	Long Tall Sally
1956	46	Teresa Brewer	Sweet Old Fashioned Girl
1956	47	Nervous Norvus	Transfusion
1956	48	Ames Brothers	It Only Hurts For A Little While
1956	49	Teresa Brewer	A Tear Fell
1956	50	Lonnie Donegan	Rock Island Line
1956	51	Dream Weavers	It's Almost Tomorrow
1956	52	Pat Boone	Friendly Persuasion (Thee I Love)
1956	53	Frank Sinatra	Hey Jealous Lover
1956	54	Eddy Heywood	Soft Summer Breeze
1956	55	Andy Williams	Canadian Sunset
1956	56	Eddie Fisher	Dungaree Doll
1956	57	George Hamilton Iv	A Rose and a Baby Ruth
1956	58	Eddie Fisher	Cindy Oh Cindy
1956	59	Jerry Vale	You Don't Know Me
1956	60	Dick Hyman	Moritat (Theme From Threepenny Opera)
1956	61	Gale Storm	Ivory Tower
1956	62	Joe Valino	Garden of Eden
1956	63	Vince Martin and the Tarriers	Cindy Oh Cindy
1956	64	Otis Williams and the Charms	Ivory Tower
1956	65	Crew Cuts	Angels in the Sky
1956	66	Mitch Miller	Song For a Summer Night

1956	67	Gale Storm	Why Do Fools Fall in Love
1956	68	Gale Storm	Teen Age Prayer
1956	69	McGuire Sisters	Picnic
1956	70	Al Hibbler	After the Lights Go Down Low
1956	71	Patti Page	Mama From the Train
1956	72	Nat King Cole	That's All There Is to That
1956	73	Kit Carson	Band of Gold
1956	74	Tony Martin	Walk Hand in Hand
1956	75	Diamonds	Why Do Fools Fall in Love
1956	76	Perry Como	Juke Box Baby
1956	77	Rusty Draper	Are You Satisfied
1956	78	Jo Stafford	It's Almost Tomorrow
1956	79	Platters	You'll Never Never Know
1956	80	Perry Como	Glendora
1956	81	Johnny Cash	I Walk the Line
1956	82	Tony Bennett	Can You Find It in Your Heart
1956	83	Pat Boone	Tutti-Frutti
1956	84	Fontane Sisters	Eddie My Love
1956	85	Don Rondo	Two Different Worlds
1956	86	Jane Powell	True Love
1956	87	Richard Hayman and Jan August	Moritat
1956	88	Nat King Cole	Night Lights
1956	89	Cadillacs	Speedoo
1956	90	Diamonds	The Church Bells May Ring
1956	91	Peggy Lee	Mr. Wonderful
1956	92	Fats Domino	My Blue Heaven
1956	93	Clyde McPhatter	Treasure of Love
1956	94	Eileen Rodgers	Miracle of Love

1956	95	Frankie Lymon and the Teenagers	I Want You to Be My Girl
1956	96	Lawrence Welk	Tonight You Belong to Me
1956	97	Chordettes	Lay Down Your Arms
1956	98	Richard Maltby	Theme From 'the Man with the Golden Arm
1956	99	Teresa Brewer	Bo Weevil
1956	100	Blue Stars	Lullaby of Birdland
		1957	
1957	1	Elvis Presley	All Shook Up
1957	2	Pat Boone	Love Letters In The Sand
1957	3	Diamonds	Little Darlin'
1957	4	Tab Hunter	Young Love
1957	5	Jimmy Dorsey	So Rare
1957	6	Pat Boone	Don't Forbid Me
1957	7	Guy Mitchell	Singing The Blues
1957	8	Sonny James	Young Love
1957	9	Elvis Presley	Too Much
1957	10	Perry Como	Round And Round
1957	11	Everly Brothers	Bye Bye Love
1957	12	Debbie Reynolds	Tammy
1957	13	Buddy Knox	Party Doll
1957	14	Elvis Presley	Teddy Bear
1957	15	Harry Belafonte	Banana Boat (Day-O)
1957	16	Elvis Presley	Jailhouse Rock
1957	17	Marty Robbins	A White Sport Coat (And A Pink Carnation)
1957	18	Del-Vikings	Come Go With Me
1957	19	Everly Brothers	Wake Up Little Susie
1957	20	Sam Cooke	You Send Me

1957	21	Coasters	Searchin'
1957	22	Chuck Berry	School Day
1957	23	Ferlin Husky	Gone
1957	24	Paul Anka	Diana
1957	25	Ricky Nelson	A Teenager's Romance
1957	26	Tarriers	The Banana Boat Song
1957	27	Jimmie Rodgers	Honeycomb
1957	28	Jerry Lee Lewis	Whole Lotta Shakin' Goin' On
1957	29	Gale Storm	Dark Moon
1957	30	Crickets	That'll Be The Day
1957	31	Charlie Gracie	Butterfly
1957	32	Frankie Laine	Moonlight Gambler
1957	33	Tommy Sands	Teenage Crush
1957	34	Johnny Mathis	It's Not For Me To Say
1957	35	Rays	Silhouettes
1957	36	Andy Williams	Butterfly
1957	37	Terry Gilkyson	Marianne
1957	38	Fats Domino	I'm Walkin'
1957	39	Johnny Mathis	Chances Are
1957	40	Nat King Cole	Send For Me
1957	41	Russ Hamilton	Rainbow
1957	42	Ricky Nelson	Be-bop Baby
1957	43	Larry Williams	Short Fat Fanny
1957	44	Jim Lowe	The Green Door
1957	45	Billy Williams	I'm Gonna Sit RIght Down And Write Myself A Letter
1957	46	Patti Page	Old Cape Cod
1957	47	Bobbettes	Mr. Lee
1957	48	Fats Domino	Blueberry Hill

13

1957	49	Del-Vikings	Whispering Bells
1957	50	Fats Domino	Blue Monday
1957	51	Johnny Mathis	Wonderful! Wonderful!
1957	52	Jane Morgan and the Troubadours	Fascination
1957	53	Bobby Helms	My Special Angel
1957	54	Billy Ward and His Dominoes	Star Dust
1957	55	Bill Justis	Raunchy
1957	56	Elvis Presley	Love Me Tender
1957	57	Harry Belafonte	Jamaica Farewell
1957	58	Pat Boone	Why Baby Why
1957	59	Betty Johnson	I Dreamed
1957	60	Buddy Knox	Hula Love
1957	61	Tune Weavers	Happy, Happy Birthday Baby
1957	62	Ivory Joe Hunter	Since I Met You Baby
1957	63	Jim Reeves	Four Walls
1957	64	Jerry Lewis	Rock-a-Bye Your Baby with a Dixie Melody
1957	65	Mantovani	Around the World
1957	66	Tony Bennett	In the Middle of an Island
1957	67	Johnnie and Joe	Over the Mountain Across the Sea
1957	68	Hilltoppers	Marianne
1957	69	Don Rondo	White Silver Sands
1957	70	Four Lads	Who Needs You
1957	71	Ames Brothers	Melodie D'Amour
1957	72	Thurston Harris	Little Bitty Pretty One
1957	73	Steve Lawrence	Party Doll
1957	74	Coasters	Young Blood

1957	75	Victor Young	Around the World
1957	76	Andy Williams	I Like Your Kind of Love
1957	77	Bonnie Guitar	Dark Moon
1957	78	Mickey and Sylvia	Love Is Strange
1957	79	Chuck Berry	Rock and Roll Music
1957	80	Little Richard	Jenny Jenny
1957	81	Pat Boone	Bernardine
1957	82	Little Richard	Keep a Knockin'
1957	83	Sal Mineo	Start Movin'
1957	84	Chuck Willis	C.C. Rider
1957	85	Gene Vincent	Lotta Lovin'
1957	86	Ernie Freeman	Raunchy
1957	87	Fats Domino	Valley of Tears
1957	88	Pat Boone	Remember You're Mine
1957	89	Guy Mitchell	Rock-a-Billy
1957	90	Margie Rayburn	I'm Available
1957	91	Larry Williams	Bony Maronie
1957	92	Harry Belafonte	Mama Look at Bubu
1957	93	Patience and Prudence	Gonna Get Along Without Ya Now
1957	94	Lavern Baker	Jim Dandy
1957	95	Marvin Rainwater	Gonna Find Me a Bluebird
1957	96	Four Coins	Shangri-La
1957	97	Rusty Draper	Freight Train
1957	98	Elvis Presley	Loving You
1957	99	Jimmy Bowen	I'm Sticking with You
1957	100	Joe Bennett and the Sparkletones	Black Slacks
		1958	
1958	1	Domenico Modugno	Volare

15

1958	2	The Everly Brothers	All I Have to Do Is Dream
1958	3	Elvis Presley	Don't
1958	4	David Seville	Witch Doctor
1958	5	Perez Prado	Patricia
1958	6	Billy Vaughn	Sail Along Silvery Moon
1958	7	Perry Como	Catch a Falling Star
1958	8	The Champs	Tequila
1958	9	Tommy Edwards	It's All in the Game
1958	10	Dean Martin	Return to Me
1958	11	Conway Twitty	It's Only Make Believe
1958	12	Sheb Wooley	The Purple People Eater
1958	13	The Everly Brothers	Bird Dog
1958	14	The Silhouettes	Get a Job
1958	15	The Elegants	Little Star
1958	16	Ricky Nelson	Stood Up
1958	17	Laurie London	He's Got the Whole World in His Hands
1958	18	The Platters	Twilight Time
1958	19	Jimmie Rodgers	Secretly
1958	20	Danny & the Juniors	At the Hop
1958	21	The Coasters	Yakety Yak
1958	22	Elvis Presley	Wear My Ring Around Your Neck
1958	23	Ricky Nelson	Poor Little Fool
1958	24	Pat Boone	A Wonderful Time Up There
1958	25	Jimmy Clanton	Just a Dream
1958	26	The McGuire Sisters	Sugartime
1958	27	Bobby Day	Rockin' Robin
1958	28	The Kingston Trio	Tom Dooley

1958	29	Chuck Berry	Sweet Little Sixteen
1958	30	Cozy Cole	Topsy Part 2
1958	31	Nat King Cole	Looking Back
1958	32	The Monotones	The Book of Love
1958	33	Tommy Dorsey Orchestra & Warren Covington	Tea For Two Cha-Cha
1958	34	Little Anthony and the Imperials	Tears on My Pillow
1958	35	Royal Teens	Short Shorts
1958	36	Jerry Lee Lewis	Great Balls of Fire
1958	37	The Chordettes	Lollipop
1958	38	Bobby Darin	Splish Splash
1958	39	Connie Francis	Who's Sorry Now?
1958	40	Jack Scott	My True Love
1958	41	Jody Reynolds	Endless Sleep
1958	42	Bobby Freeman	Do You Want to Dance
1958	43	The Kalin Twins	When
1958	44	The Teddy Bears	To Know Him Is to Love Him
1958	45	Pat Boone	April Love
1958	46	Duane Eddy	Rebel-'Rouser
1958	47	The Crescendos	Oh, Julie
1958	48	The Diamonds	The Stroll
1958	49	Elvis Presley	Hard Headed Woman
1958	50	Buddy Holly & The Crickets	Peggy Sue
1958	51	Don Gibson	Oh Lonesome Me
1958	52	The Big Bopper	Chantilly Lace
1958	53	Rick Nelson	Lonesome Town
1958	54	Frank Sinatra	All the Way
1958	55	Elvis Presley	One Night

1958	56	Robin Luke	Susie Darlin'
1958	57	Four Preps	26 Miles
1958	58	Earl Grant	The End
1958	59	Jimmie Rodgers	Kisses Sweeter Than Wine
1958	60	The Playmates	Beep Beep
1958	61	Mitch Miller	March From the River Kwai and Colonel Bogey March
1958	62	Everly Brothers	Problems
1958	63	Bobby Darin	Queen of the Hop
1958	64	Will Glahe	Liechtensteiner Polka
1958	65	Elvis Presley	I Got Stung
1958	66	Andy Williams	Are You Sincere
1958	67	Ricky Nelson	I Got a Feeling
1958	68	The Poni-Tails	Born Too Late
1958	69	Johnny Otis Show	Willie and the Hand Jive
1958	70	Four Preps	Big Man
1958	71	Crickets	Oh Boy
1958	72	Chuck Willis	What Am I Living For
1958	73	Chuck Berry	Johnny B Goode
1958	74	Eddie Cochran	Summertime Blues
1958	75	Roger Williams	Near You
1958	76	Peggy Lee	Fever
1958	77	Ed Townsend	For Your Love
1958	78	Paul Anka	You Are My Destiny
1958	79	Art and Dotty Todd	Chanson D'Amour
1958	80	Lou Monte	Lazy Mary
1958	81	Johnny Cash	Ballad of a Teenage Queen
1958	82	Pat Boone	It's Too Soon to Know
1958	83	Jimmy McCracklin	The Walk

1958	84	Perry Como	Kewpie Doll
1958	85	George Hamilton IV	Why Don't They Understand
1958	86	Frankie Avalon	DeDe Dinah
1958	87	Pat Boone	Sugar Moon
1958	88	Everly Brothers	Devoted to You
1958	89	Chantels	Maybe
1958	90	Kathy Linden	Billy
1958	91	Johnny Cash	Guess Things Happen That Way
1958	92	The Olympics	Western Movies
1958	93	Roy Hamilton	Don't Let Go
1958	94	Hollywood Flames	Buzz-Buzz-Buzz
1958	95	Jerry Lee Lewis	Breathless
1958	96	Jan and Arnie	Jennie Lee
1958	97	The Royaltones	Poor Boy
1958	98	Marty Robbins	The Story of My Life
1958	99	Frankie Avalon	I'll Wait for You
1958	100	Frankie Avalon	Ginger Bread
		1959	
1959	1	Johnny Horton	The Battle Of New Orleans
1959	2	Bobby Darin	Mack The Knife
1959	3	Lloyd Price	Personality
1959	4	Frankie Avalon	Venus
1959	5	Paul Anka	Lonely Boy
1959	6	Bobby Darin	Dream Lover
1959	7	Browns	The Three Bells
1959	8	Fleetwoods	Come Softly To Me
1959	9	Wilbert Harrison	Kansas City
1959	10	Fleetwoods	Mr. Blue

1959	11	Santo and Johnny	Sleep Walk
1959	12	Paul Anka	Put Your Head On My Shoulder
1959	13	Lloyd Price	Stagger Lee
1959	14	Ritchie Valens	Donna
1959	15	Dodie Stevens	Pink Shoelaces
1959	16	Platters	Smoke Gets In Your Eyes
1959	17	The Coasters	Charlie Brown
1959	18	Martin Denny	Quiet Village
1959	19	Carl Dobkins Jr.	My Heart Is An Open Book
1959	20	Everly Brothers	('Til) I Kissed You
1959	21	Phil Phillips and The Twilights	Sea Of Love
1959	22	Dave "Baby" Cortez	The Happy Organ
1959	23	Lloyd Price	I'm Gonna Get Married
1959	24	Impalas	Sorry (I Ran All The Way Home)
1959	25	Dion and The Belmonts	A Teenager In Love
1959	26	Crests	16 Candles
1959	27	Brook Benton	It's Just A Matter Of Time
1959	28	Connie Francis	Lipstick On Your Collar
1959	29	Drifters	There Goes My Baby
1959	30	Elvis Presley	A Big Hunk O' Love
1959	31	Johnny and The Hurricanes	Red River Rock
1959	32	Stonewall Jackson	Waterloo
1959	33	Sammy Turner	Lavender Blue (Dilly Dilly)
1959	34	Elvis Presley	(Now And Then There's) A Fool Such As I
1959	35	The Virtues	Guitar Boogie Shuffle
1959	36	Sandy Nelson	Teen Beat

1959	37	Edward Burns and Connie Stevens	Kookie Kookie (Lend Me Your Comb)
1959	38	Thomas Wayne	Tragedy
1959	39	Connie Francis	My Happiness
1959	40	Freddie Cannon	Tallahassee Lassie
1959	41	Fabian	Tiger
1959	42	Ricky Nelson	Never Be Anyone Else But You
1959	43	Della Reese	Don't You Know
1959	44	Elvis Presley	I Need Your Love Tonight
1959	45	Dinah Washington	What A Diff'rence A Day Makes
1959	46	Bill Parsons	The All American Boy
1959	47	Jerry Wallace	Primrose Lane
1959	48	David Seville and The Chipmunks	Alvin's Harmonica
1959	49	Andy Williams	Lonely Street
1959	50	Ray Charles	What'd I Say
1959	51	Sarah Vaughan	Broken-hearted Melody
1959	52	Franck Pourcel	Only You
1959	53	Billy Grammer	Gotta Travel On
1959	54	Coasters	Poison Ivy
1959	55	Fabian	Turn Me Loose
1959	56	Jackie Wilson	Lonely Teardrops
1959	57	Andy Williams	Hawaiian Wedding Song
1959	58	Duane Eddy	Forty Miles Of Bad Road
1959	59	Frankie Avalon	Just Ask Your Heart
1959	60	Travis and Bob	Tell Him No
1959	61	Connie Francis	Frankie
1959	62	The Bell Notes	I've Had It

1959	63	Lavern Baker	I Cried A Tear
1959	64	Platters	Enchanted
1959	65	Skyliners	Since I Don't Have You
1959	66	Ray Anthony	Peter Gunn Theme
1959	67	David Seville and The Chipmunks	The Chipmunk Song
1959	68	Fats Domino	I Want To Walk You Home
1959	69	Fiestas	So Fine
1959	70	Frankie Avalon	Bobby Sox To Stockings
1959	71	Wink Martindale	Deck Of Cards
1959	72	Clyde Mcphatter	A Lover's Question
1959	73	Flamingos	I Only Have Eyes For You
1959	74	Ricky Nelson	It's Late
1959	75	Chris Barber's Jazz Band	Petite Fleur
1959	76	Annette Funicello	Tall Paul
1959	77	Kingston Trio	The Tijuana Jail
1959	78	Ricky Nelson	Just A Little Too Much
1959	79	Jack Scott	Goodbye Baby
1959	80	Coasters	Along Came Jones
1959	81	Tommy Dee and Carol Kay	Three Stars
1959	82	Frankie Avalon	A Boy Without A Girl
1959	83	Ricky Nelson	Sweeter Than You
1959	84	Skip and Flip	It Was I
1959	85	Kathy Linden	Goodbye, Jimmy, Goodbye
1959	86	Reg Owens Orch.	Manhattan Spiritual
1959	87	Brook Benton	Endlessly
1959	88	Guy Mitchell	Heartaches By The Number
1959	89	Frankie Ford	Sea Cruise
1959	90	Jackie Wilson	That's Why
1959	91	Falcons	You're So Fine

1959	92	Bobby Rydell	Kissin' Time
1959	93	Elvis Presley	My Wish Came True
1959	94	Ivo Robic	Morgen
1959	95	Jan and Dean	Baby Talk
1959	96	Preston Epps	Bongo Rock
1959	97	Everly Brothers	Take A Message To Mary
1959	98	Mormon Tabernacle Choir	Battle Hymn Of The Republic
1959	99	Ernie Fields Orchestra	In The Mood
1959	100	Paul Evans and The Curls	(Seven Little Girls) Sitting In The Back Seat

ARTISTS

This Section is simply a listing of the songs sorted alphabetically by Artist Name. When the songs are performed by the same artist, they are then sorted by year and then chart position.

Year	#	Artist	Song Title
1955	21	Al Hibbler	Unchained Melody
1956	70	Al Hibbler	After the Lights Go Down Low
1952	9	Al Martino	Here In My Heart
1950	16	Ames Brothers	Sentimental Me
1950	23	Ames Brothers	Rag Mop
1950	27	Ames Brothers	Can Anyone Explain?
1953	5	Ames Brothers	You, You, You
1955	27	Ames Brothers	The Naughty Lady Of Shady Lane
1956	48	Ames Brothers	It Only Hurts For A Little While
1957	71	Ames Brothers	Melodie D'Amour
1951	28	Ames Brothers and Les Brown	Undecided
1950	17	Andrews Sisters and Gordon Jenkins	I Wanna Be Loved
1950	19	Andrews Sisters and Gordon Jenkins	I Can Dream, Can't I

25

1956	55	Andy Williams	Canadian Sunset
1957	36	Andy Williams	Butterfly
1957	76	Andy Williams	I Like Your Kind of Love
1958	66	Andy Williams	Are You Sincere
1959	49	Andy Williams	Lonely Street
1959	57	Andy Williams	Hawaiian Wedding Song
1959	76	Annette Funicello	Tall Paul
1950	3	Anton Karas	Third Man Theme
1954	10	Archie Bleyer	Hernando's Hideaway
1958	79	Art and Dotty Todd	Chanson D'Amour
1955	23	Art Mooney	Honey Babe
1957	59	Betty Johnson	I Dreamed
1956	21	Bill Doggett	Honky Tonk
1954	26	Bill Haley and His Comets	Shake, Rattle And Roll
1955	2	Bill Haley and His Comets	Rock Around The Clock
1956	33	Bill Haley and His Comets	See You Later Alligator
1955	6	Bill Hayes	The Ballad Of Davy Crockett
1957	55	Bill Justis	Raunchy
1959	46	Bill Parsons	The All American Boy
1950	24	Bill Snyder	Bewitched
1950	28	Billy Eckstine	My Foolish Heart
1951	25	Billy Eckstine	I Apologize
1959	53	Billy Grammer	Gotta Travel On
1955	12	Billy Vaughn	Melody Of Love
1958	6	Billy Vaughn	Sail Along Silvery Moon
1957	54	Billy Ward and His Dominoes	Star Dust
1957	45	Billy Williams	I'm Gonna Sit RIght Down And Write Myself A Letter

1950	29	Bing Crosby	Dear Hearts And Gentle People
1956	44	Bing Crosby and Grace Kelly	True Love
1956	100	Blue Stars	Lullaby of Birdland
1957	47	Bobbettes	Mr. Lee
1958	38	Bobby Darin	Splish Splash
1958	63	Bobby Darin	Queen of the Hop
1959	2	Bobby Darin	Mack The Knife
1959	6	Bobby Darin	Dream Lover
1958	27	Bobby Day	Rockin' Robin
1958	42	Bobby Freeman	Do You Want to Dance
1957	53	Bobby Helms	My Special Angel
1959	92	Bobby Rydell	Kissin' Time
1957	77	Bonnie Guitar	Dark Moon
1959	27	Brook Benton	It's Just A Matter Of Time
1959	87	Brook Benton	Endlessly
1959	7	Browns	The Three Bells
1956	30˙	Buchanan and Goodman	The Flying Saucer
1958	50	Buddy Holly & The Crickets	Peggy Sue
1957	13	Buddy Knox	Party Doll
1957	60	Buddy Knox	Hula Love
1956	89	Cadillacs	Speedoo
1959	19	Carl Dobkins Jr.	My Heart Is An Open Book
1956	18	Carl Perkins	Blue Suede Shoes
1956	32	Cathy Carr	Ivory Tower
1958	89	Chantels	Maybe
1957	31	Charlie Gracie	Butterfly
1955	18	Chordettes	Mr. Sandman
1956	37	Chordettes	Born To Be With You

1956	97	Chordettes	Lay Down Your Arms
1959	75	Chris Barber's Jazz Band	Petite Fleur
1957	22	Chuck Berry	School Day
1957	79	Chuck Berry	Rock and Roll Music
1958	29	Chuck Berry	Sweet Little Sixteen
1958	73	Chuck Berry	Johnny B Goode
1957	84	Chuck Willis	C.C. Rider
1958	72	Chuck Willis	What Am I Living For
1956	93	Clyde McPhatter	Treasure of Love
1959	72	Clyde McPhatter	A Lover's Question
1957	21	Coasters	Searchin'
1957	74	Coasters	Young Blood
1959	54	Coasters	Poison Ivy
1959	80	Coasters	Along Came Jones
1958	39	Connie Francis	Who's Sorry Now?
1959	28	Connie Francis	Lipstick On Your Collar
1959	39	Connie Francis	My Happiness
1959	61	Connie Francis	Frankie
1958	11	Conway Twitty	It's Only Make Believe
1958	30	Cozy Cole	Topsy Part 2
1955	11	Crazy Otto	Crazy Otto Medley I and II
1959	26	Crests	16 Candles
1954	4	Crew Cuts	Sh-Boom
1956	65	Crew Cuts	Angels in the Sky
1957	30	Crickets	That'll Be The Day
1958	71	Crickets	Oh Boy
1958	20	Danny & the Juniors	At the Hop
1959	22	Dave "Baby" Cortez	The Happy Organ
1958	4	David Seville	Witch Doctor

1959	48	David Seville and The Chipmunks	Alvin's Harmonica
1959	67	David Seville and The Chipmunks	The Chipmunk Song
1954	16	Dean Martin	That's Amore
1956	9	Dean Martin	Memories Are Made Of This
1958	10	Dean Martin	Return to Me
1957	12	Debbie Reynolds	Tammy
1951	22	Debbie Reynolds and **Carleton Carpenter**	Aba Daba Honeymoon
1951	24	Del Wood	Down Yonder
1959	43	Della Reese	Don't You Know
1957	18	Del-Vikings	Come Go With Me
1957	49	Del-Vikings	Whispering Bells
1956	75	Diamonds	Why Do Fools Fall in Love
1956	90	Diamonds	The Church Bells May Ring
1957	3	Diamonds	Little Darlin'
1956	60	Dick Hyman	Moritat (Theme From Threepenny Opera)
1951	18	Dinah Shore	Sweet Violets
1959	45	Dinah Washington	What A Diff'rence A Day Makes
1959	25	Dion and The Belmonts	A Teenager In Love
1959	15	Dodie Stevens	Pink Shoelaces
1958	1	Domenico Modugno	Volare
1956	38	Don Cherry	Band Of Gold
1952	26	Don Cornell	I'm Yours
1952	27	Don Cornell	I'll Walk Alone
1954	23	Don Cornell	Hold My Hand

1958	51	Don Gibson	Oh Lonesome Me
1956	43	Don Robertson	The Happy Whistler
1956	85	Don Rondo	Two Different Worlds
1957	69	Don Rondo	White Silver Sands
1952	17	Doris Day	A Guy Is A Guy
1954	9	Doris Day	Secret Love
1954	20	Doris Day	If I Give My Heart To You
1956	7	Doris Day	Whatever Will Be Will Be (Que Sera Sera)
1956	51	Dream Weavers	It's Almost Tomorrow
1959	29	Drifters	There Goes My Baby
1958	46	Duane Eddy	Rebel-'Rouser
1959	58	Duane Eddy	Forty Miles Of Bad Road
1958	58	Earl Grant	The End
1953	29	Eartha Kitt	C'est Si Bon
1958	77	Ed Townsend	For Your Love
1958	74	Eddie Cochran	Summertime Blues
1953	4	Eddie Fisher	I'm Walking Behind You
1953	28	Eddie Fisher	With These Hands
1954	6	Eddie Fisher	Oh! My Pa-pa
1954	13	Eddie Fisher	I Need You Now
1956	56	Eddie Fisher	Dungaree Doll
1956	58	Eddie Fisher	Cindy Oh Cindy
1952	7	Eddie Fisher and Hugo Winterhalter	Wish You Were Here
1952	12	Eddie Fisher and Hugo Winterhalter	Anytime
1952	20	Eddie Fisher and Hugo Winterhalter	I'm Yours

1952	28	Eddie Fisher and Hugo Winterhalter	Tell Me Why
1956	17	Eddie Heywood and Hugo Winterhalter	Canadian Sunset
1956	54	Eddy Heywood	Soft Summer Breeze
1951	16	Eddy Howard	(It's No) Sin
1959	37	Edward Burns and Connie Stevens	Kookie Kookie (Lend Me Your Comb)
1950	11	Eileen Barton	If I Knew You Were Coming I'd've Baked A Cake
1956	94	Eileen Rodgers	Miracle of Love
1952	14	Ella Mae Morse	Blacksmith Blues
1956	1	Elvis Presley	Heartbreak Hotel
1956	2	Elvis Presley	Don't Be Cruel
1956	8	Elvis Presley	Hound Dog
1956	14	Elvis Presley	I Want You, I Need You, I Love You
1956	15	Elvis Presley	Love Me Tender
1957	1	Elvis Presley	All Shook Up
1957	9	Elvis Presley	Too Much
1957	14	Elvis Presley	Teddy Bear
1957	16	Elvis Presley	Jailhouse Rock
1957	56	Elvis Presley	Love Me Tender
1957	98	Elvis Presley	Loving You
1958	3	Elvis Presley	Don't
1958	22	Elvis Presley	Wear My Ring Around Your Neck
1958	49	Elvis Presley	Hard Headed Woman
1958	55	Elvis Presley	One Night

1958	65	Elvis Presley	I Got Stung
1959	30	Elvis Presley	A Big Hunk O' Love
1959	34	Elvis Presley	(Now And Then There's) A Fool Such As I
1959	44	Elvis Presley	I Need Your Love Tonight
1959	93	Elvis Presley	My Wish Came True
1959	99	Ernie Fields Orchestra	In The Mood
1957	86	Ernie Freeman	Raunchy
1957	11	Everly Brothers	Bye Bye Love
1957	19	Everly Brothers	Wake Up Little Susie
1958	62	Everly Brothers	Problems
1958	88	Everly Brothers	Devoted to You
1959	20	Everly Brothers	('Til) I Kissed You
1959	97	Everly Brothers	Take A Message To Mary
1959	41	Fabian	Tiger
1959	55	Fabian	Turn Me Loose
1959	91	Falcons	You're So Fine
1956	25	Fats Domino	I'm In Love Again
1956	41	Fats Domino	Blueberry Hill
1956	92	Fats Domino	My Blue Heaven
1957	38	Fats Domino	I'm Walkin'
1957	48	Fats Domino	Blueberry Hill
1957	50	Fats Domino	Blue Monday
1957	87	Fats Domino	Valley of Tears
1959	68	Fats Domino	I Want To Walk You Home
1957	23	Ferlin Husky	Gone
1955	22	Fess Parker	The Ballad Of Davy Crockett
1959	69	Fiestas	So Fine
1959	73	Flamingos	I Only Have Eyes For You

1959	8	Fleetwoods	Come Softly To Me
1959	10	Fleetwoods	Mr. Blue
1955	15	Fontaine Sisters	Hearts Of Stone
1956	84	Fontaine Sisters	Eddie My Love
1952	13	Four Aces	Tell Me Why
1954	8	Four Aces	Three Coins In The Fountain
1954	29	Four Aces	Stranger In Paradise
1955	7	Four Aces	Love Is A Many Splendored Thing
1951	21	Four Aces and Al Alberts	(It's No) Sin
1957	96	Four Coins	Shangri-La
1954	7	Four Knights	I Get So Lonely
1955	17	Four Lads	Moments To Remember
1956	20	Four Lads	No, Not Much
1956	29	Four Lads	Standing On The Corner
1957	70	Four Lads	Who Needs You
1958	57	Four Preps	26 Miles
1958	70	Four Preps	Big Man
1959	52	Franck Pourcel	Only You
1953	12	Frank Chacksfield	Ebb Tide
1953	27	Frank Chacksfield	Limelight (Terry's Theme)
1954	11	Frank Sinatra	Young At Heart
1955	14	Frank Sinatra	Learnin' The Blues
1956	53	Frank Sinatra	Hey Jealous Lover
1958	54	Frank Sinatra	All the Way
1954	17	Frank Weir	The Happy Wanderer
1958	86	Frankie Avalon	DeDe Dinah
1958	99	Frankie Avalon	I'll Wait for You
1958	100	Frankie Avalon	Ginger Bread

1959	4	Frankie Avalon	Venus
1959	59	Frankie Avalon	Just Ask Your Heart
1959	70	Frankie Avalon	Bobby Sox To Stockings
1959	82	Frankie Avalon	A Boy Without A Girl
1959	89	Frankie Ford	Sea Cruise
1950	30	Frankie Laine	Cry Of The Wild Goose
1951	11	Frankie Laine	Jezebel
1951	23	Frankie Laine	Rose, Rose I Love You
1952	19	Frankie Laine	High Noon
1953	10	Frankie Laine	I Believe
1957	32	Frankie Laine	Moonlight Gambler
1953	23	Frankie Laine and Jimmy Boyd	Tell Me A Story
1956	28	Frankie Lymon and The Teenagers	Why Do Fools Fall In Love
1956	95	Frankie Lymon and the Teenagers	I Want You to Be My Girl
1959	40	Freddie Cannon	Tallahassee Lassie
1956	61	Gale Storm	Ivory Tower
1956	67	Gale Storm	Why Do Fools Fall in Love
1956	68	Gale Storm	Teen Age Prayer
1957	29	Gale Storm	Dark Moon
1950	4	Gary and Bing Crosby	Sam's Song
1950	5	Gary and Bing Crosby	Simple Melody
1953	17	Gaylords	Tell Me You're Mine
1954	15	Gaylords	The Little Shoemaker
1956	27	Gene Vincent	Be-Bop-A-Lula
1957	85	Gene Vincent	Lotta Lovin'

1956	31	George Cates	Moonglow And Theme From Picnic
1956	57	George Hamilton Iv	A Rose and a Baby Ruth
1958	85	George Hamilton IV	Why Don't They Understand
1952	11	Georgia Gibbs	Kiss Of Fire
1955	10	Georgia Gibbs	Dance With Me Henry
1955	16	Georgia Gibbs	Tweedle Dee
1955	26	Gisele Mackenzie	Hard To Get
1956	5	Gogi Grant	The Wayward Wind
1950	22	Gordon Jenkins	My Foolish Heart
1950	26	Gordon Jenkins	Bewitched
1950	1	Gordon Jenkins and The Weavers	Goodnight Irene
1950	13	Gordon Jenkins and The Weavers	Tzena, Tzena, Tzena
1950	7	Guy Lombardo	Third Man Theme
1956	40	Guy Mitchell	Singing The Blues
1957	7	Guy Mitchell	Singing The Blues
1957	89	Guy Mitchell	Rock-a-Billy
1959	88	Guy Mitchell	Heartaches By The Number
1951	15	Guy Mitchell and Mitch Miller	My Heart Cries For You
1951	20	Guy Mitchell and Mitch Miller	My Truly, Truly Fair
1957	15	Harry Belafonte	Banana Boat (Day-O)
1957	57	Harry Belafonte	Jamaica Farewell
1957	92	Harry Belafonte	Mama Look at Bubu
1952	29	Hilltoppers	Trying

1953	16	Hilltoppers	P.S. I Love You
1957	68	Hilltoppers	Marianne
1958	94	Hollywood Flames	Buzz-Buzz-Buzz
1959	24	Impalas	Sorry (I Ran All The Way Home)
1959	94	Ivo Robic	Morgen
1957	62	Ivory Joe Hunter	Since I Met You Baby
1958	40	Jack Scott	My True Love
1959	79	Jack Scott	Goodbye Baby
1959	56	Jackie Wilson	Lonely Teardrops
1959	90	Jackie Wilson	That's Why
1958	96	Jan and Arnie	Jennie Lee
1959	95	Jan and Dean	Baby Talk
1957	52	Jane Morgan and the Troubadours	Fascination
1956	86	Jane Powell	True Love
1955	28	Jaye P. Morgan	That's All I Want From You
1957	28	Jerry Lee Lewis	Whole Lotta Shakin' Goin' On
1958	36	Jerry Lee Lewis	Great Balls of Fire
1958	95	Jerry Lee Lewis	Breathless
1957	64	Jerry Lewis	Rock-a-Bye Your Baby with a Dixie Melody
1956	59	Jerry Vale	You Don't Know Me
1959	47	Jerry Wallace	Primrose Lane
1956	19	Jim Lowe	The Green Door
1957	44	Jim Lowe	The Green Door
1957	63	Jim Reeves	Four Walls
1957	27	Jimmie Rodgers	Honeycomb

1958	19	Jimmie Rodgers	Secretly
1958	59	Jimmie Rodgers	Kisses Sweeter Than Wine
1957	99	Jimmy Bowen	I'm Sticking with You
1958	25	Jimmy Clanton	Just a Dream
1957	5	Jimmy Dorsey	So Rare
1958	83	Jimmy McCracklin	The Walk
1952	4	Jo Stafford	You Belong To Me
1952	15	Jo Stafford	Jambalaya
1954	5	Jo Stafford	Make Love To Me
1956	78	Jo Stafford	It's Almost Tomorrow
1955	19	Joan Weber	Let Me Go Lover
1958	41	Jody Reynolds	Endless Sleep
1957	100	Joe Bennett and the Sparkletones	Black Slacks
1956	62	Joe Valino	Garden of Eden
1957	67	Johnnie and Joe	Over the Mountain Across the Sea
1952	3	Johnnie Ray	Cry
1952	18	Johnnie Ray	The Little White Cloud That Cried
1952	24	Johnnie Ray	Walkin' My Baby Back Home
1952	30	Johnnie Ray	Please, Mr. Sun
1956	23	Johnnie Ray	Just Walking In The Rain
1959	31	Johnny and The Hurricanes	Red River Rock
1956	81	Johnny Cash	I Walk the Line
1958	81	Johnny Cash	Ballad of a Teenage Queen
1958	91	Johnny Cash	Guess Things Happen That Way

1959	1	Johnny Horton	The Battle Of New Orleans
1957	34	Johnny Mathis	It's Not For Me To Say
1957	39	Johnny Mathis	Chances Are
1957	51	Johnny Mathis	Wonderful! Wonderful!
1958	69	Johnny Otis Show	Willie and the Hand Jive
1952	22	Johnny Standley	It's In The Book
1953	25	Joni James	Why Don't You Believe Me
1953	26	Joni James	Your Cheating Heart
1953	30	Joni James	Have You Heard?
1953	18	Julius La Rosa	Eh Cumpari
1953	24	June Valli	Crying In The Chapel
1958	90	Kathy Linden	Billy
1959	85	Kathy Linden	Goodbye, Jimmy, Goodbye
1950	12	Kay Starr	Bonaparte's Retreat
1952	2	Kay Starr	Wheel Of Fortune
1954	21	Kay Starr	If You Love Me (Really Love Me)
1956	10	Kay Starr	Rock And Roll Waltz
1959	77	Kingston Trio	The Tijuana Jail
1956	73	Kit Carson	Band of Gold
1954	1	Kitty Kallen	Little Things Mean A Lot
1954	28	Kitty Kallen	In The Chapel In The Moonlight
1957	43	Larry Williams	Short Fat Fanny
1957	91	Larry Williams	Bony Maronie
1958	17	Laurie London	He's Got the Whole World in His Hands
1957	94	Lavern Baker	Jim Dandy
1959	63	Lavern Baker	I Cried A Tear

1956	96	Lawrence Welk	Tonight You Belong to Me
1952	1	Leroy Anderson	Blue Tango
1951	30	Les Baxter	Because Of You
1953	7	Les Baxter	April In Portugal
1955	5	Les Baxter	Unchained Melody
1956	6	Les Baxter	The Poor People Of Paris
1952	25	Les Paul	Meet Mr. Callaghan
1951	3	Les Paul and Mary Ford	How High The Moon
1951	13	Les Paul and Mary Ford	Mockin' Bird Hill
1951	19	Les Paul and Mary Ford	The World Is Waiting For The Sunrise
1953	2	Les Paul and Mary Ford	Vaya Con Dios
1958	34	Little Anthony and the Imperials	Tears on My Pillow
1956	45	Little Richard	Long Tall Sally
1957	80	Little Richard	Jenny Jenny
1957	82	Little Richard	Keep a Knockin'
1959	3	Lloyd Price	Personality
1959	13	Lloyd Price	Stagger Lee
1959	23	Lloyd Price	I'm Gonna Get Married
1956	50	Lonnie Donegan	Rock Island Line
1958	80	Lou Monte	Lazy Mary
1957	65	Mantovani	Around the World
1957	90	Margie Rayburn	I'm Available
1951	5	Mario Lanza	Be My Love
1951	9	Mario Lanza	Loveliest Night Of The Year
1959	18	Martin Denny	Quiet Village
1957	17	Marty Robbins	A White Sport Coat (And A Pink Carnation)

1958	98	Marty Robbins	The Story of My Life
1957	95	Marvin Rainwater	Gonna Find Me a Bluebird
1955	8	McGuire Sisters	Sincerely
1956	69	McGuire Sisters	Picnic
1957	78	Mickey and Sylvia	Love Is Strange
1952	21	Mills Brothers	Glow Worm
1955	3	Mitch Miller	The Yellow Rose Of Texas
1956	66	Mitch Miller	Song For a Summer Night
1958	61	Mitch Miller	March From the River Kwai and Colonel Bogey March
1959	98	Mormon Tabernacle Choir	Battle Hymn Of The Republic
1956	11	Morris Stoloff	Moonglow And Theme From "Picnic"
1950	2	Nat King Cole	Mona Lisa
1951	1	Nat King Cole	Too Young
1953	13	Nat King Cole	Pretend
1954	18	Nat King Cole	Answer Me My Love
1955	20	Nat King Cole	A Blossom Fell
1956	72	Nat King Cole	That's All There Is to That
1956	88	Nat King Cole	Night Lights
1957	40	Nat King Cole	Send For Me
1958	31	Nat King Cole	Looking Back
1956	3	Nelson Riddle	Lisbon Antigua
1956	47	Nervous Norvus	Transfusion
1956	64	Otis Williams and the Charms	Ivory Tower
1955	9	Pat Boone	Ain't That A Shame
1956	13	Pat Boone	I Almost Lost My Mind
1956	34	Pat Boone	I'll Be Home

1956	52	Pat Boone	Friendly Persuasion (Thee I Love)
1956	83	Pat Boone	Tutti-Frutti
1957	2	Pat Boone	Love Letters In The Sand
1957	6	Pat Boone	Don't Forbid Me
1957	58	Pat Boone	Why Baby Why
1957	81	Pat Boone	Bernadine
1957	88	Pat Boone	Remember You're Mine
1958	24	Pat Boone	A Wonderful Time Up There
1958	45	Pat Boone	April Love
1958	82	Pat Boone	It's Too Soon to Know
1958	87	Pat Boone	Sugar Moon
1956	26	Patience and Prudence	Tonight You Belong To Me
1957	93	Patience and Prudence	Gonna Get Along Without Ya Now
1950	18	Patti Page	Tennessee Waltz
1950	21	Patti Page	All My Love
1951	10	Patti Page	Tennessee Waltz
1951	14	Patti Page	Mockin' Bird Hill
1951	26	Patti Page	Would I Love You
1952	8	Patti Page	I Went To Your Wedding
1953	3	Patti Page	Doggie In The Window
1954	14	Patti Page	Cross Over The Bridge
1954	24	Patti Page	Changing Partners
1956	24	Patti Page	Allegheny Moon
1956	71	Patti Page	Mama From the Train
1957	46	Patti Page	Old Cape Cod
1957	24	Paul Anka	Diana
1958	78	Paul Anka	You Are My Destiny

1959	5	Paul Anka	Lonely Boy
1959	12	Paul Anka	Put Your Head On My Shoulder
1959	100	Paul Evans and The Curls	(Seven Little Girls) Sitting In The Back Seat
1953	11	Pee Wee Hunt	Oh
1952	23	Pee Wee King	Slow Poke
1956	91	Peggy Lee	Mr. Wonderful
1958	76	Peggy Lee	Fever
1952	10	Percy Faith	Delicado
1953	1	Percy Faith	Song From Moulin Rouge
1955	1	Perez Prado	Cherry Pink And Apple Blossom White
1958	5	Perez Prado	Patricia
1950	25	Perry Como	Hoop-Dee-Doo
1951	8	Perry Como	If
1953	8	Perry Como	No Other Love
1953	9	Perry Como	Don't Let The Stars Get In Your Eyes
1953	21	Perry Como	Say You're Mine Again
1954	2	Perry Como	Wanted
1954	25	Perry Como	Papa Loves Mambo
1955	25	Perry Como	Ko Ko Mo
1956	16	Perry Como	Hot Diggity
1956	39	Perry Como	More
1956	76	Perry Como	Juke Box Baby
1956	80	Perry Como	Glendora
1957	10	Perry Como	Round And Round
1958	7	Perry Como	Catch a Falling Star
1958	84	Perry Como	Kewpie Doll

1951	27	Perry Como and The Fontaine Sisters	You're Just In Love
1950	15	Phil Harris	The Thing
1951	29	Phil Harris	The Thing
1959	21	Phil Phillips and The Twilights	Sea Of Love
1955	29	Platters	Only You
1956	4	Platters	My Prayer
1956	12	Platters	The Great Pretender
1956	36	Platters	Magic Touch
1956	79	Platters	You'll Never Never Know
1959	16	Platters	Smoke Gets In Your Eyes
1959	64	Platters	Enchanted
1959	96	Preston Epps	Bongo Rock
1954	22	Ralph Marterie	Skokiaan
1953	22	Ray Anthony	Dragnet
1959	66	Ray Anthony	Peter Gunn Theme
1959	50	Ray Charles	What'd I Say
1957	35	Rays	Silhouettes
1950	8	Red Foley	Chattanoogie Shoe Shine Boy
1959	86	Reg Owens Orch.	Manhattan Spiritual
1953	14	Richard Hayman	Ruby
1956	87	Richard Hayman and Jan August	Moritat
1956	98	Richard Maltby	Theme From 'the Man with the Golden Arm
1958	53	Rick Nelson	Lonesome Town
1957	25	Ricky Nelson	A Teenager's Romance
1957	42	Ricky Nelson	Be-bop Baby
1958	16	Ricky Nelson	Stood Up

1958	23	Ricky Nelson	Poor Little Fool
1958	67	Ricky Nelson	I Got a Feeling
1959	42	Ricky Nelson	Never Be Anyone Else But You
1959	74	Ricky Nelson	It's Late
1959	78	Ricky Nelson	Just A Little Too Much
1959	83	Ricky Nelson	Sweeter Than You
1959	14	Ritchie Valens	Donna
1958	56	Robin Luke	Susie Darlin'
1955	4	Roger Williams	Autumn Leaves
1958	75	Roger Williams	Near You
1951	4	Rosemary Clooney	Come On-a My House
1952	6	Rosemary Clooney	Half As Much
1952	16	Rosemary Clooney	Botch-a-me
1954	3	Rosemary Clooney	Hey There
1954	12	Rosemary Clooney	This Ole House
1958	93	Roy Hamilton	Don't Let Go
1958	35	Royal Teens	Short Shorts
1957	41	Russ Hamilton	Rainbow
1956	77	Rusty Draper	Are You Satisfied
1957	97	Rusty Draper	Freight Train
1957	83	Sal Mineo	Start Movin'
1957	20	Sam Cooke	You Send Me
1950	9	Sammy Kaye	Harbor Lights
1950	10	Sammy Kaye and Don Cornell	It Isn't Fair
1959	33	Sammy Turner	Lavender Blue (Dilly Dilly)
1959	36	Sandy Nelson	Teen Beat
1956	42	Sanford Clark	The Fool

1959	11	Santo and Johnny	Sleep Walk
1959	51	Sarah Vaughan	Broken-hearted Melody
1958	12	Sheb Wooley	The Purple People Eater
1953	20	Silvana Mangano	Anna
1959	84	Skip and Flip	It Was I
1959	65	Skyliners	Since I Don't Have You
1955	30	Somethin' Smith and The Redheads	It's A Sin To Tell A Lie
1957	8	Sonny James	Young Love
1953	15	Stan Freberg	St. George And The Dragonet
1957	73	Steve Lawrence	Party Doll
1959	32	Stonewall Jackson	Waterloo
1957	4	Tab Hunter	Young Love
1957	26	Tarriers	The Banana Boat Song
1955	13	Tennessee Ernie Ford	Sixteen Tons
1955	24	Tennessee Ernie Ford	The Ballad Of Davy Crockett
1956	22	Tennessee Ernie Ford	Sixteen Tons
1950	20	Tennessee Ernie Ford and Kay Starr	I'll Never Be Free
1950	6	Teresa Brewer	Music, Music, Music
1953	6	Teresa Brewer	Till I Waltz Again With You
1956	46	Teresa Brewer	Sweet Old Fashioned Girl
1956	49	Teresa Brewer	A Tear Fell
1956	99	Teresa Brewer	Bo Weevil
1957	37	Terry Gilkyson	Marianne
1959	62	The Bell Notes	I've Had It
1958	52	The Big Bopper	Chantilly Lace
1958	8	The Champs	Tequila

1958	37	The Chordettes	Lollipop
1958	21	The Coasters	Yakety Yak
1959	17	The Coasters	Charlie Brown
1958	47	The Crescendos	Oh, Julie
1958	48	The Diamonds	The Stroll
1958	15	The Elegants	Little Star
1958	2	The Everly Brothers	All I Have to Do Is Dream
1958	13	The Everly Brothers	Bird Dog
1958	43	The Kalin Twins	When
1958	28	The Kingston Trio	Tom Dooley
1958	26	The McGuire Sisters	Sugartime
1958	32	The Monotones	The Book of Love
1958	92	The Olympics	Western Movies
1958	18	The Platters	Twilight Time
1958	60	The Playmates	Beep Beep
1958	68	The Poni-Tails	Born Too Late
1958	97	The Royaltones	Poor Boy
1958	14	The Silhouettes	Get a Job
1958	44	The Teddy Bears	To Know Him Is to Love Him
1959	35	The Virtues	Guitar Boogie Shuffle
1959	38	Thomas Wayne	Tragedy
1957	72	Thurston Harris	Little Bitty Pretty One
1959	81	Tommy Dee and Carol Kay	Three Stars
1958	33	Tommy Dorsey Orchestra & Warren Covington	Tea For Two Cha-Cha
1958	9	Tommy Edwards	It's All in the Game
1957	33	Tommy Sands	Teenage Crush
1951	2	Tony Bennett	Because Of You

1951	7	Tony Bennett	Cold, Cold Heart
1953	19	Tony Bennett	Rags To Riches
1954	19	Tony Bennett	Stranger In Paradise
1954	27	Tony Bennett	Rags To Riches
1956	82	Tony Bennett	Can You Find It in Your Heart
1957	66	Tony Bennett	In the Middle of an Island
1950	14	Tony Martin	There's No Tomorrow
1951	12	Tony Martin	I Get Ideas
1954	30	Tony Martin	Here
1956	74	Tony Martin	Walk Hand in Hand
1959	60	Travis and Bob	Tell Him No
1957	61	Tune Weavers	Happy, Happy Birthday Baby
1951	17	Vaughn Monroe	Sound Off
1952	5	Vera Lynn	Auf Wiederseh'n, Sweetheart
1956	35	Vic Damone	On The Street Where You Live
1957	75	Victor Young	Around the World
1956	63	Vince Martin and the Tarriers	Cindy Oh Cindy
1951	6	Weavers	On Top Of Old Smoky
1959	9	Wilbert Harrison	Kansas City
1958	64	Will Glahe	Liechtensteiner Polka
1959	71	Wink Martindale	Deck Of Cards

SONG TITLES

In this Section, I have sorted the Top 100 Master List by Song Titles. The songs are listed first alphabetically, then by year and then by rankings. By doing this some amazing information is gleaned. First, many times the same song will show up on the list by different artists. In 26 cases where this occurred, both versions (or in 2 instances, all three versions) charted in the same year. The only exception to this was "Only You" which charted in 1955 for The Platters and in 1959 for Franck Pourcel. In addition, eight songs charted twice for the same artists in different years. Another interesting note is the listing of Tutti-Frutti. This song is known today as the breakout hit of Little Richard. Yet, his name does not appear on the chart next to title. Instead the version that charted on the Top 100 list for 1956 was performed by Pat Boone- a version essentially forgotten today (Little Richard's version made it to #17 on the weekly pop charts and was ranked #43 in Rolling Stones list of the 500 Greatest Songs of All Time).

Year	#	Song Title	Artist
1951	16	(It's No) Sin	Eddy Howard
1951	21	(It's No) Sin	Four Aces and Al Alberts
1959	34	(Now And Then There's) A Fool Such As I	Elvis Presley

1959	100	(Seven Little Girls) Sitting In The Back Seat	Paul Evans and The Curls
1959	20	('Til) I Kissed You	Everly Brothers
1959	26	16 Candles	Crests
1958	57	26 Miles	Four Preps
1959	30	A Big Hunk O' Love	Elvis Presley
1955	20	A Blossom Fell	Nat King Cole
1959	82	A Boy Without A Girl	Frankie Avalon
1952	17	A Guy Is A Guy	Doris Day
1959	72	A Lover's Question	Clyde Mcphatter
1956	57	A Rose and a Baby Ruth	George Hamilton Iv
1956	49	A Tear Fell	Teresa Brewer
1959	25	A Teenager In Love	Dion and The Belmonts
1957	25	A Teenager's Romance	Ricky Nelson
1957	17	A White Sport Coat (And A Pink Carnation)	Marty Robbins
1958	24	A Wonderful Time Up There	Pat Boone
1951	22	Aba Daba Honeymoon	Debbie Reynolds and Carleton Carpenter
1956	70	After the Lights Go Down Low	Al Hibbler
1955	9	Ain't That A Shame	Pat Boone
1958	2	All I Have to Do Is Dream	The Everly Brothers
1950	21	All My Love	Patti Page
1957	1	All Shook Up	Elvis Presley
1958	54	All the Way	Frank Sinatra
1956	24	Allegheny Moon	Patti Page
1959	80	Along Came Jones	Coasters
1959	48	Alvin's Harmonica	David Seville and The Chipmunks
1956	65	Angels in the Sky	Crew Cuts

1953	20	Anna	Silvana Mangano
1954	18	Answer Me My Love	Nat King Cole
1952	12	Anytime	Eddie Fisher and Hugo Winterhalter
1953	7	April In Portugal	Les Baxter
1958	45	April Love	Pat Boone
1956	77	Are You Satisfied	Rusty Draper
1958	66	Are You Sincere	Andy Williams
1957	65	Around the World	Mantovani
1957	75	Around the World	Victor Young
1958	20	At the Hop	Danny & the Juniors
1952	5	Auf Wiederseh'n, Sweetheart	Vera Lynn
1955	4	Autumn Leaves	Roger Williams
1959	95	Baby Talk	Jan and Dean
1958	81	Ballad of a Teenage Queen	Johnny Cash
1957	15	Banana Boat (Day-O)	Harry Belafonte
1956	38	Band Of Gold	Don Cherry
1956	73	Band of Gold	Kit Carson
1959	98	Battle Hymn Of The Republic	Mormon Tabernacle Choir
1951	5	Be My Love	Mario Lanza
1957	42	Be-bop Baby	Ricky Nelson
1956	27	Be-Bop-A-Lula	Gene Vincent
1951	2	Because Of You	Tony Bennett
1951	30	Because Of You	Les Baxter
1958	60	Beep Beep	The Playmates
1957	81	Bernardine	Pat Boone
1950	24	Bewitched	Bill Snyder
1950	26	Bewitched	Gordon Jenkins

1958	70	Big Man	Four Preps
1958	90	Billy	Kathy Linden
1958	13	Bird Dog	The Everly Brothers
1957	100	Black Slacks	Joe Bennett and the Sparkletones
1952	14	Blacksmith Blues	Ella Mae Morse
1957	50	Blue Monday	Fats Domino
1956	18	Blue Suede Shoes	Carl Perkins
1952	1	Blue Tango	Leroy Anderson
1956	41	Blueberry Hill	Fats Domino
1957	48	Blueberry Hill	Fats Domino
1956	99	Bo Weevil	Teresa Brewer
1959	70	Bobby Sox To Stockings	Frankie Avalon
1950	12	Bonaparte's Retreat	Kay Starr
1959	96	Bongo Rock	Preston Epps
1957	91	Bony Maronie	Larry Williams
1956	37	Born To Be With You	Chordettes
1958	68	Born Too Late	The Poni-Tails
1952	16	Botch-a-me	Rosemary Clooney
1958	95	Breathless	Jerry Lee Lewis
1959	51	Broken-hearted Melody	Sarah Vaughan
1957	31	Butterfly	Charlie Gracie
1957	36	Butterfly	Andy Williams
1958	94	Buzz-Buzz-Buzz	Hollywood Flames
1957	11	Bye Bye Love	Everly Brothers
1957	84	C.C. Rider	Chuck Willis
1950	27	Can Anyone Explain?	Ames Brothers
1956	82	Can You Find It in Your Heart	Tony Bennett
1956	17	Canadian Sunset	Eddie Heywood and Hugo Winterhalter

1956	55	Canadian Sunset	Andy Williams
1958	7	Catch a Falling Star	Perry Como
1953	29	C'est Si Bon	Eartha Kitt
1957	39	Chances Are	Johnny Mathis
1954	24	Changing Partners	Patti Page
1958	79	Chanson D'Amour	Art and Dotty Todd
1958	52	Chantilly Lace	The Big Bopper
1959	17	Charlie Brown	The Coasters
1950	8	Chattanoogie Shoe Shine Boy	Red Foley
1955	1	Cherry Pink And Apple Blossom White	Perez Prado
1956	58	Cindy Oh Cindy	Eddie Fisher
1956	63	Cindy Oh Cindy	Vince Martin and the Tarriers
1951	7	Cold, Cold Heart	Tony Bennett
1957	18	Come Go With Me	Del-Vikings
1951	4	Come On-a My House	Rosemary Clooney
1959	8	Come Softly To Me	Fleetwoods
1955	11	Crazy Otto Medley I and II	Crazy Otto
1954	14	Cross Over The Bridge	Patti Page
1952	3	Cry	Johnnie Ray
1950	30	Cry Of The Wild Goose	Frankie Laine
1953	24	Crying In The Chapel	June Valli
1955	10	Dance With Me Henry	Georgia Gibbs
1957	29	Dark Moon	Gale Storm
1957	77	Dark Moon	Bonnie Guitar
1950	29	Dear Hearts And Gentle People	Bing Crosby
1959	71	Deck Of Cards	Wink Martindale

1958	86	DeDe Dinah	Frankie Avalon
1952	10	Delicado	Percy Faith
1958	88	Devoted to You	Everly Brothers
1957	24	Diana	Paul Anka
1958	42	Do You Want to Dance	Bobby Freeman
1953	3	Doggie In The Window	Patti Page
1959	14	Donna	Ritchie Valens
1958	3	Don't	Elvis Presley
1956	2	Don't Be Cruel	Elvis Presley
1957	6	Don't Forbid Me	Pat Boone
1958	93	Don't Let Go	Roy Hamilton
1953	9	Don't Let The Stars Get In Your Eyes	Perry Como
1959	43	Don't You Know	Della Reese
1951	24	Down Yonder	Del Wood
1953	22	Dragnet	Ray Anthony
1959	6	Dream Lover	Bobby Darin
1956	56	Dungaree Doll	Eddie Fisher
1953	12	Ebb Tide	Frank Chacksfield
1956	84	Eddie My Love	Fontane Sisters
1953	18	Eh Cumpari	Julius La Rosa
1959	64	Enchanted	Platters
1958	41	Endless Sleep	Jody Reynolds
1959	87	Endlessly	Brook Benton
1957	52	Fascination	Jane Morgan and the Troubadours
1958	76	Fever	Peggy Lee
1958	77	For Your Love	Ed Townsend
1959	58	Forty Miles Of Bad Road	Duane Eddy
1957	63	Four Walls	Jim Reeves

1959	61	Frankie	Connie Francis
1957	97	Freight Train	Rusty Draper
1956	52	Friendly Persuasion (Thee I Love)	Pat Boone
1956	62	Garden of Eden	Joe Valino
1958	14	Get a Job	The Silhouettes
1958	100	Ginger Bread	Frankie Avalon
1956	80	Glendora	Perry Como
1952	21	Glow Worm	Mills Brothers
1957	23	Gone	Ferlin Husky
1957	95	Gonna Find Me a Bluebird	Marvin Rainwater
1957	93	Gonna Get Along Without Ya Now	Patience and Prudence
1959	79	Goodbye Baby	Jack Scott
1959	85	Goodbye, Jimmy, Goodbye	Kathy Linden
1950	1	Goodnight Irene	Gordon Jenkins and The Weavers
1959	53	Gotta Travel On	Billy Grammer
1958	36	Great Balls of Fire	Jerry Lee Lewis
1958	91	Guess Things Happen That Way	Johnny Cash
1959	35	Guitar Boogie Shuffle	The Virtues
1952	6	Half As Much	Rosemary Clooney
1957	61	Happy, Happy Birthday Baby	Tune Weavers
1950	9	Harbor Lights	Sammy Kaye
1958	49	Hard Headed Woman	Elvis Presley
1955	26	Hard To Get	Gisele Mackenzie
1953	30	Have You Heard?	Joni James
1959	57	Hawaiian Wedding Song	Andy Williams
1959	88	Heartaches By The Number	Guy Mitchell

1956	1	Heartbreak Hotel	Elvis Presley
1955	15	Hearts Of Stone	Fontaine Sisters
1954	30	Here	Tony Martin
1952	9	Here In My Heart	Al Martino
1954	10	Hernando's Hideaway	Archie Bleyer
1958	17	He's Got the Whole World in His Hands	Laurie London
1956	53	Hey Jealous Lover	Frank Sinatra
1954	3	Hey There	Rosemary Clooney
1952	19	High Noon	Frankie Laine
1954	23	Hold My Hand	Don Cornell
1955	23	Honey Babe	Art Mooney
1957	27	Honeycomb	Jimmie Rodgers
1956	21	Honky Tonk	Bill Doggett
1950	25	Hoop-Dee-Doo	Perry Como
1956	16	Hot Diggity	Perry Como
1956	8	Hound Dog	Elvis Presley
1951	3	How High The Moon	Les Paul and Mary Ford
1957	60	Hula Love	Buddy Knox
1956	13	I Almost Lost My Mind	Pat Boone
1951	25	I Apologize	Billy Eckstine
1953	10	I Believe	Frankie Laine
1950	19	I Can Dream, Can't I	Andrews Sisters and Gordon Jenkins
1959	63	I Cried A Tear	Lavern Baker
1957	59	I Dreamed	Betty Johnson
1951	12	I Get Ideas	Tony Martin
1954	7	I Get So Lonely	Four Knights
1958	67	I Got a Feeling	Ricky Nelson
1958	65	I Got Stung	Elvis Presley

1957	76	I Like Your Kind of Love	Andy Williams
1954	13	I Need You Now	Eddie Fisher
1959	44	I Need Your Love Tonight	Elvis Presley
1959	73	I Only Have Eyes For You	Flamingos
1956	81	I Walk the Line	Johnny Cash
1950	17	I Wanna Be Loved	Andrews Sisters and Gordon Jenkins
1959	68	I Want To Walk You Home	Fats Domino
1956	95	I Want You to Be My Girl	Frankie Lymon and the Teenagers
1956	14	I Want You, I Need You, I Love You	Elvis Presley
1952	8	I Went To Your Wedding	Patti Page
1951	8	If	Perry Como
1954	20	If I Give My Heart To You	Doris Day
1950	11	If I Knew You Were Coming I'd've Baked A Cake	Eileen Barton
1954	21	If You Love Me (Really Love Me)	Kay Starr
1956	34	I'll Be Home	Pat Boone
1950	20	I'll Never Be Free	Tennessee Ernie Ford and Kay Starr
1958	99	I'll Wait for You	Frankie Avalon
1952	27	I'll Walk Alone	Don Cornell
1957	90	I'm Available	Margie Rayburn
1959	23	I'm Gonna Get Married	Lloyd Price
1957	45	I'm Gonna Sit RIght Down And Write Myself A Letter	Billy Williams
1956	25	I'm In Love Again	Fats Domino
1957	99	I'm Sticking with You	Jimmy Bowen
1957	38	I'm Walkin'	Fats Domino

1953	4	I'm Walking Behind You	Eddie Fisher
1952	20	I'm Yours	Eddie Fisher and Hugo Winterhalter
1952	26	I'm Yours	Don Cornell
1954	28	In The Chapel In The Moonlight	Kitty Kallen
1957	66	In the Middle of an Island	Tony Bennett
1959	99	In The Mood	Ernie Fields Orchestra
1950	10	It Isn't Fair	Sammy Kaye and Don Cornell
1956	48	It Only Hurts For A Little While	Ames Brothers
1959	84	It Was I	Skip and Flip
1955	30	It's A Sin To Tell A Lie	Somethin' Smith and The Redheads
1958	9	It's All in the Game	Tommy Edwards
1956	51	It's Almost Tomorrow	Dream Weavers
1956	78	It's Almost Tomorrow	Jo Stafford
1952	22	It's In The Book	Johnny Standley
1959	27	It's Just A Matter Of Time	Brook Benton
1959	74	It's Late	Ricky Nelson
1957	34	It's Not For Me To Say	Johnny Mathis
1958	11	It's Only Make Believe	Conway Twitty
1958	82	It's Too Soon to Know	Pat Boone
1959	62	I've Had It	The Bell Notes
1956	32	Ivory Tower	Cathy Carr
1956	61	Ivory Tower	Gale Storm
1956	64	Ivory Tower	Otis Williams and the Charms
1957	16	Jailhouse Rock	Elvis Presley
1957	57	Jamaica Farewell	Harry Belafonte

1952	15	Jambalaya	Jo Stafford
1958	96	Jennie Lee	Jan and Arnie
1957	80	Jenny Jenny	Little Richard
1951	11	Jezebel	Frankie Laine
1957	94	Jim Dandy	Lavern Baker
1958	73	Johnny B Goode	Chuck Berry
1956	76	Juke Box Baby	Perry Como
1958	25	Just a Dream	Jimmy Clanton
1959	78	Just A Little Too Much	Ricky Nelson
1959	59	Just Ask Your Heart	Frankie Avalon
1956	23	Just Walking In The Rain	Johnnie Ray
1959	9	Kansas City	Wilbert Harrison
1957	82	Keep a Knockin'	Little Richard
1958	84	Kewpie Doll	Perry Como
1952	11	Kiss Of Fire	Georgia Gibbs
1958	59	Kisses Sweeter Than Wine	Jimmie Rodgers
1959	92	Kissin' Time	Bobby Rydell
1955	25	Ko Ko Mo	Perry Como
1959	37	Kookie Kookie (Lend Me Your Comb)	Edward Burns and Connie Stevens
1959	33	Lavender Blue (Dilly Dilly)	Sammy Turner
1956	97	Lay Down Your Arms	Chordettes
1958	80	Lazy Mary	Lou Monte
1955	14	Learnin' The Blues	Frank Sinatra
1955	19	Let Me Go Lover	Joan Weber
1958	64	Liechtensteiner Polka	Will Glahe
1953	27	Limelight (Terry's Theme)	Frank Chacksfield
1959	28	Lipstick On Your Collar	Connie Francis
1956	3	Lisbon Antigua	Nelson Riddle
1957	72	Little Bitty Pretty One	Thurston Harris

1957	3	Little Darlin'	Diamonds
1958	15	Little Star	The Elegants
1954	1	Little Things Mean A Lot	Kitty Kallen
1958	37	Lollipop	The Chordettes
1959	5	Lonely Boy	Paul Anka
1959	49	Lonely Street	Andy Williams
1959	56	Lonely Teardrops	Jackie Wilson
1958	53	Lonesome Town	Rick Nelson
1956	45	Long Tall Sally	Little Richard
1958	31	Looking Back	Nat King Cole
1957	85	Lotta Lovin'	Gene Vincent
1955	7	Love Is A Many Splendored Thing	Four Aces
1957	78	Love Is Strange	Mickey and Sylvia
1957	2	Love Letters In The Sand	Pat Boone
1956	15	Love Me Tender	Elvis Presley
1957	56	Love Me Tender	Elvis Presley
1951	9	Loveliest Night Of The Year	Mario Lanza
1957	98	Loving You	Elvis Presley
1956	100	Lullaby of Birdland	Blue Stars
1959	2	Mack The Knife	Bobby Darin
1956	36	Magic Touch	Platters
1954	5	Make Love To Me	Jo Stafford
1956	71	Mama From the Train	Patti Page
1957	92	Mama Look at Bubu	Harry Belafonte
1959	86	Manhattan Spiritual	Reg Owens Orch.
1958	61	March From the River Kwai and Colonel Bogey March	Mitch Miller
1957	37	Marianne	Terry Gilkyson
1957	68	Marianne	Hilltoppers

1958	89	Maybe	Chantels
1952	25	Meet Mr. Callaghan	Les Paul
1957	71	Melodie D'Amour	Ames Brothers
1955	12	Melody Of Love	Billy Vaughn
1956	9	Memories Are Made Of This	Dean Martin
1956	94	Miracle of Love	Eileen Rodgers
1951	13	Mockin' Bird Hill	Les Paul and Mary Ford
1951	14	Mockin' Bird Hill	Patti Page
1955	17	Moments To Remember	Four Lads
1950	2	Mona Lisa	Nat King Cole
1956	11	Moonglow And Theme From "Picnic"	Morris Stoloff
1956	31	Moonglow And Theme From Picnic	George Cates
1957	32	Moonlight Gambler	Frankie Laine
1956	39	More	Perry Como
1959	94	Morgen	Ivo Robic
1956	87	Moritat	Richard Hayman and Jan August
1956	60	Moritat (Theme From Threepenny Opera)	Dick Hyman
1956	91	Mr. Wonderful	Peggy Lee
1959	10	Mr. Blue	Fleetwoods
1957	47	Mr. Lee	Bobbettes
1955	18	Mr. Sandman	Chordettes
1950	6	Music, Music, Music	Teresa Brewer
1956	92	My Blue Heaven	Fats Domino
1950	22	My Foolish Heart	Gordon Jenkins
1950	28	My Foolish Heart	Billy Eckstine
1959	39	My Happiness	Connie Francis

1951	15	My Heart Cries For You	Guy Mitchell and Mitch Miller
1959	19	My Heart Is An Open Book	Carl Dobkins Jr.
1956	4	My Prayer	Platters
1957	53	My Special Angel	Bobby Helms
1958	40	My True Love	Jack Scott
1951	20	My Truly, Truly Fair	Guy Mitchell and Mitch Miller
1959	93	My Wish Came True	Elvis Presley
1958	75	Near You	Roger Williams
1959	42	Never Be Anyone Else But You	Ricky Nelson
1956	88	Night Lights	Nat King Cole
1953	8	No Other Love	Perry Como
1956	20	No, Not Much	Four Lads
1953	11	Oh	Pee Wee Hunt
1958	71	Oh Boy	Crickets
1958	51	Oh Lonesome Me	Don Gibson
1954	6	Oh! My Pa-pa	Eddie Fisher
1958	47	Oh, Julie	The Crescendos
1957	46	Old Cape Cod	Patti Page
1956	35	On The Street Where You Live	Vic Damone
1951	6	On Top Of Old Smoky	Weavers
1958	55	One Night	Elvis Presley
1955	29	Only You	Platters
1959	52	Only You	Franck Pourcel
1957	67	Over the Mountain Across the Sea	Johnnie and Joe
1953	16	P.S. I Love You	Hilltoppers
1954	25	Papa Loves Mambo	Perry Como

1957	13	Party Doll	Buddy Knox
1957	73	Party Doll	Steve Lawrence
1958	5	Patricia	Perez Prado
1958	50	Peggy Sue	Buddy Holly & The Crickets
1959	3	Personality	Lloyd Price
1959	66	Peter Gunn Theme	Ray Anthony
1959	75	Petite Fleur	Chris Barber's Jazz Band
1956	69	Picnic	McGuire Sisters
1959	15	Pink Shoelaces	Dodie Stevens
1952	30	Please, Mr. Sun	Johnnie Ray
1959	54	Poison Ivy	Coasters
1958	97	Poor Boy	The Royaltones
1958	23	Poor Little Fool	Ricky Nelson
1953	13	Pretend	Nat King Cole
1959	47	Primrose Lane	Jerry Wallace
1958	62	Problems	Everly Brothers
1959	12	Put Your Head On My Shoulder	Paul Anka
1958	63	Queen of the Hop	Bobby Darin
1959	18	Quiet Village	Martin Denny
1950	23	Rag Mop	Ames Brothers
1953	19	Rags To Riches	Tony Bennett
1954	27	Rags To Riches	Tony Bennett
1957	41	Rainbow	Russ Hamilton
1957	55	Raunchy	Bill Justis
1957	86	Raunchy	Ernie Freeman
1958	46	Rebel-'Rouser	Duane Eddy
1959	31	Red River Rock	Johnny and The Hurricanes
1957	88	Remember You're Mine	Pat Boone
1958	10	Return to Me	Dean Martin

1957	79	Rock and Roll Music	Chuck Berry
1956	10	Rock And Roll Waltz	Kay Starr
1955	2	Rock Around The Clock	Bill Haley and His Comets
1956	50	Rock Island Line	Lonnie Donegan
1957	89	Rock-a-Billy	Guy Mitchell
1957	64	Rock-a-Bye Your Baby with a Dixie Melody	Jerry Lewis
1958	27	Rockin' Robin	Bobby Day
1951	23	Rose, Rose I Love You	Frankie Laine
1957	10	Round And Round	Perry Como
1953	14	Ruby	Richard Hayman
1958	6	Sail Along Silvery Moon	Billy Vaughn
1950	4	Sam's Song	Gary and Bing Crosby
1953	21	Say You're Mine Again	Perry Como
1957	22	School Day	Chuck Berry
1959	89	Sea Cruise	Frankie Ford
1959	21	Sea Of Love	Phil Phillips and The Twilights
1957	21	Searchin'	Coasters
1954	9	Secret Love	Doris Day
1958	19	Secretly	Jimmie Rodgers
1956	33	See You Later Alligator	Bill Haley and His Comets
1957	40	Send For Me	Nat King Cole
1950	16	Sentimental Me	Ames Brothers
1954	26	Shake, Rattle And Roll	Bill Haley and His Comets
1957	96	Shangri-La	Four Coins
1954	4	Sh-Boom	Crew Cuts
1957	43	Short Fat Fanny	Larry Williams
1958	35	Short Shorts	Royal Teens
1957	35	Silhouettes	Rays

1950	5	Simple Melody	Gary and Bing Crosby
1959	65	Since I Don't Have You	Skyliners
1957	62	Since I Met You Baby	Ivory Joe Hunter
1955	8	Sincerely	McGuire Sisters
1956	40	Singing The Blues	Guy Mitchell
1957	7	Singing The Blues	Guy Mitchell
1955	13	Sixteen Tons	Tennessee Ernie Ford
1956	22	Sixteen Tons	Tennessee Ernie Ford
1954	22	Skokiaan	Ralph Marterie
1959	11	Sleep Walk	Santo and Johnny
1952	23	Slow Poke	Pee Wee King
1959	16	Smoke Gets In Your Eyes	Platters
1959	69	So Fine	Fiestas
1957	5	So Rare	Jimmy Dorsey
1956	54	Soft Summer Breeze	Eddy Heywood
1956	66	Song For a Summer Night	Mitch Miller
1953	1	Song From Moulin Rouge	Percy Faith
1959	24	Sorry (I Ran All The Way Home)	Impalas
1951	17	Sound Off	Vaughn Monroe
1956	89	Speedoo	Cadillacs
1958	38	Splish Splash	Bobby Darin
1953	15	St. George And The Dragonet	Stan Freberg
1959	13	Stagger Lee	Lloyd Price
1956	29	Standing On The Corner	Four Lads
1957	54	Star Dust	Billy Ward and His Dominoes
1957	83	Start Movin'	Sal Mineo
1958	16	Stood Up	Ricky Nelson

1954	19	Stranger In Paradise	Tony Bennett
1954	29	Stranger In Paradise	Four Aces
1958	87	Sugar Moon	Pat Boone
1958	26	Sugartime	The McGuire Sisters
1958	74	Summertime Blues	Eddie Cochran
1958	56	Susie Darlin'	Robin Luke
1958	29	Sweet Little Sixteen	Chuck Berry
1956	46	Sweet Old Fashioned Girl	Teresa Brewer
1951	18	Sweet Violets	Dinah Shore
1959	83	Sweeter Than You	Ricky Nelson
1959	97	Take A Message To Mary	Everly Brothers
1959	40	Tallahassee Lassie	Freddie Cannon
1959	76	Tall Paul	Annette Funicello
1957	12	Tammy	Debbie Reynolds
1958	33	Tea For Two Cha-Cha	Tommy Dorsey Orchestra & Warren Covington
1958	34	Tears on My Pillow	Little Anthony and the Imperials
1957	14	Teddy Bear	Elvis Presley
1956	68	Teen Age Prayer	Gale Storm
1959	36	Teen Beat	Sandy Nelson
1957	33	Teenage Crush	Tommy Sands
1959	60	Tell Him No	Travis and Bob
1953	23	Tell Me A Story	Frankie Laine and Jimmy Boyd
1952	13	Tell Me Why	Four Aces
1952	28	Tell Me Why	Eddie Fisher and Hugo Winterhalter
1953	17	Tell Me You're Mine	Gaylords
1950	18	Tennessee Waltz	Patti Page

1951	10	Tennessee Waltz	Patti Page
1958	8	Tequila	The Champs
1957	30	That'll Be The Day	Crickets
1955	28	That's All I Want From You	Jaye P. Morgan
1956	72	That's All There Is to That	Nat King Cole
1954	16	That's Amore	Dean Martin
1959	90	That's Why	Jackie Wilson
1959	46	The All American Boy	Bill Parsons
1955	6	The Ballad Of Davy Crockett	Bill Hayes
1955	22	The Ballad Of Davy Crockett	Fess Parker
1955	24	The Ballad Of Davy Crockett	Tennessee Ernie Ford
1957	26	The Banana Boat Song	Tarriers
1959	1	The Battle Of New Orleans	Johnny Horton
1958	32	The Book of Love	The Monotones
1959	67	The Chipmunk Song	David Seville and The Chipmunks
1956	90	The Church Bells May Ring	Diamonds
1958	58	The End	Earl Grant
1956	30	The Flying Saucer	Buchanan and Goodman
1956	42	The Fool	Sanford Clark
1956	12	The Great Pretender	Platters
1956	19	The Green Door	Jim Lowe
1957	44	The Green Door	Jim Lowe
1959	22	The Happy Organ	Dave "Baby" Cortez
1954	17	The Happy Wanderer	Frank Weir
1956	43	The Happy Whistler	Don Robertson
1954	15	The Little Shoemaker	Gaylords
1952	18	The Little White Cloud That Cried	Johnnie Ray

1955	27	The Naughty Lady Of Shady Lane	Ames Brothers
1956	6	The Poor People Of Paris	Les Baxter
1958	12	The Purple People Eater	Sheb Wooley
1958	98	The Story of My Life	Marty Robbins
1958	48	The Stroll	The Diamonds
1950	15	The Thing	Phil Harris
1951	29	The Thing	Phil Harris
1959	7	The Three Bells	Browns
1959	77	The Tijuana Jail	Kingston Trio
1958	83	The Walk	Jimmy McCracklin
1956	5	The Wayward Wind	Gogi Grant
1951	19	The World Is Waiting For The Sunrise	Les Paul and Mary Ford
1955	3	The Yellow Rose Of Texas	Mitch Miller
1956	98	Theme From 'the Man with the Golden Arm	Richard Maltby
1959	29	There Goes My Baby	Drifters
1950	14	There's No Tomorrow	Tony Martin
1950	3	Third Man Theme	Anton Karas
1950	7	Third Man Theme	Guy Lombardo
1954	12	This Ole House	Rosemary Clooney
1954	8	Three Coins In The Fountain	Four Aces
1959	81	Three Stars	Tommy Dee and Carol Kay
1959	41	Tiger	Fabian
1953	6	Till I Waltz Again With You	Teresa Brewer
1958	44	To Know Him Is to Love Him	The Teddy Bears
1958	28	Tom Dooley	The Kingston Trio
1956	26	Tonight You Belong To Me	Patience and Prudence
1956	96	Tonight You Belong to Me	Lawrence Welk

1957	9	Too Much	Elvis Presley
1951	1	Too Young	Nat King Cole
1958	30	Topsy Part 2	Cozy Cole
1959	38	Tragedy	Thomas Wayne
1956	47	Transfusion	Nervous Norvus
1956	93	Treasure of Love	Clyde McPhatter
1956	44	True Love	Bing Crosby and Grace Kelly
1956	86	True Love	Jane Powell
1952	29	Trying	Hilltoppers
1959	55	Turn Me Loose	Fabian
1956	83	Tutti-Frutti	Pat Boone
1955	16	Tweedle Dee	Georgia Gibbs
1958	18	Twilight Time	The Platters
1956	85	Two Different Worlds	Don Rondo
1950	13	Tzena, Tzena, Tzena	Gordon Jenkins and The Weavers
1955	5	Unchained Melody	Les Baxter
1955	21	Unchained Melody	Al Hibbler
1951	28	Undecided	Ames Brothers and Les Brown
1957	87	Valley of Tears	Fats Domino
1953	2	Vaya Con Dios	Les Paul and Mary Ford
1959	4	Venus	Frankie Avalon
1958	1	Volare	Domenico Modugno
1957	19	Wake Up Little Susie	Everly Brothers
1956	74	Walk Hand in Hand	Tony Martin
1952	24	Walkin' My Baby Back Home	Johnnie Ray
1954	2	Wanted	Perry Como
1959	32	Waterloo	Stonewall Jackson

1958	22	Wear My Ring Around Your Neck	Elvis Presley
1958	92	Western Movies	The Olympics
1959	45	What A Diff'rence A Day Makes	Dinah Washington
1958	72	What Am I Living For	Chuck Willis
1959	50	What'd I Say	Ray Charles
1956	7	Whatever Will Be Will Be (Que Sera Sera)	Doris Day
1952	2	Wheel Of Fortune	Kay Starr
1958	43	When	The Kalin Twins
1957	49	Whispering Bells	Del-Vikings
1957	69	White Silver Sands	Don Rondo
1957	70	Who Needs You	Four Lads
1957	28	Whole Lotta Shakin' Goin' On	Jerry Lee Lewis
1958	39	Who's Sorry Now?	Connie Francis
1957	58	Why Baby Why	Pat Boone
1956	28	Why Do Fools Fall In Love	Frankie Lymon and The Teenagers
1956	67	Why Do Fools Fall in Love	Gale Storm
1956	75	Why Do Fools Fall in Love	Diamonds
1958	85	Why Don't They Understand	George Hamilton IV
1953	25	Why Don't You Believe Me	Joni James
1958	69	Willie and the Hand Jive	Johnny Otis Show
1952	7	Wish You Were Here	Eddie Fisher and Hugo Winterhalter
1958	4	Witch Doctor	David Seville
1953	28	With These Hands	Eddie Fisher
1957	51	Wonderful! Wonderful!	Johnny Mathis
1951	26	Would I Love You	Patti Page

1958	21	Yakety Yak	The Coasters
1958	78	You Are My Destiny	Paul Anka
1952	4	You Belong To Me	Jo Stafford
1956	59	You Don't Know Me	Jerry Vale
1957	20	You Send Me	Sam Cooke
1953	5	You, You, You	Ames Brothers
1956	79	You'll Never Never Know	Platters
1954	11	Young At Heart	Frank Sinatra
1957	74	Young Blood	Coasters
1957	4	Young Love	Tab Hunter
1957	8	Young Love	Sonny James
1953	26	Your Cheating Heart	Joni James
1951	27	You're Just In Love	Perry Como and The Fontane Sisters
1959	91	You're So Fine	Falcons

THE MEN

Men dominated the charts. Of the 580 songs that made the Master List, 332 were by male solo artists (57.2%). The remaining 42.6% were split between women and groups. The 333 songs were performed by a total of 163 men. Of course, four men were responsible for 60 of those hits (Elvis Presley, Perry Como, Pat Boone and Ricky Nelson).

The results are slightly skewed due to how the charts list artists. The 1950's was the tail end of the big band era. Many of the chart hits are performed by big bands and orchestras. In fact, at least 23 of the songs were performed by band leaders (Archie Bleyer, Art Mooney, Billy Vaughn, Eddy Howard, Frank Chacksfield, Frank Weir, George Cates, Jimmy Dorsey, Lawrence Welk, Larry Anderson, Les Baxter, Mitch Miller, Morris Stoloff, Nelson Riddle, Pee Wee Hunt, Percy Faith, Perez Prado, Ralph Marterie, Ray Anthony, Richard Hayman, Vaughn Monroe, Victor Young, and Will Glahe). As was the style of the day, the orchestras and big bands are often listed only by the conductor's name.

It should be noted that this list only includes songs where the artist is listed as a soloist. Many performers also appear as part of a group or duet for songs on the master list. Those songs have not been included in this list and would in many cases increase the overall hit count for the artist.

Year	#	Artist	Song Title
1955	21	Al Hibbler	Unchained Melody
1956	70	Al Hibbler	After the Lights Go Down Low
1952	9	Al Martino	Here In My Heart
1956	55	Andy Williams	Canadian Sunset
1957	36	Andy Williams	Butterfly
1957	76	Andy Williams	I Like Your Kind of Love
1958	66	Andy Williams	Are You Sincere
1959	49	Andy Williams	Lonely Street
1959	57	Andy Williams	Hawaiian Wedding Song
1950	3	Anton Karas	Third Man Theme
1954	10	Archie Bleyer	Hernando's Hideaway
1955	23	Art Mooney	Honey Babe
1956	21	Bill Doggett	Honky Tonk
1955	6	Bill Hayes	The Ballad Of Davy Crockett
1957	55	Bill Justis	Raunchy
1959	46	Bill Parsons	The All American Boy
1950	24	Bill Snyder	Bewitched
1950	28	Billy Eckstine	My Foolish Heart
1951	25	Billy Eckstine	I Apologize
1959	53	Billy Grammer	Gotta Travel On
1955	12	Billy Vaughn	Melody Of Love
1958	6	Billy Vaughn	Sail Along Silvery Moon
1957	45	Billy Williams	I'm Gonna Sit RIght Down And Write Myself A Letter
1950	29	Bing Crosby	Dear Hearts And Gentle People

1958	38	Bobby Darin	Splish Splash
1958	63	Bobby Darin	Queen of the Hop
1959	2	Bobby Darin	Mack The Knife
1959	6	Bobby Darin	Dream Lover
1958	27	Bobby Day	Rockin' Robin
1958	42	Bobby Freeman	Do You Want to Dance
1957	53	Bobby Helms	My Special Angel
1959	92	Bobby Rydell	Kissin' Time
1959	27	Brook Benton	It's Just A Matter Of Time
1959	87	Brook Benton	Endlessly
1957	13	Buddy Knox	Party Doll
1957	60	Buddy Knox	Hula Love
1959	19	Carl Dobkins Jr.	My Heart Is An Open Book
1956	18	Carl Perkins	Blue Suede Shoes
1957	31	Charlie Gracie	Butterfly
1957	22	Chuck Berry	School Day
1957	79	Chuck Berry	Rock and Roll Music
1958	29	Chuck Berry	Sweet Little Sixteen
1958	73	Chuck Berry	Johnny B Goode
1957	84	Chuck Willis	C.C. Rider
1958	72	Chuck Willis	What Am I Living For
1956	93	Clyde McPhatter	Treasure of Love
1959	72	Clyde Mcphatter	A Lover's Question
1958	11	Conway Twitty	It's Only Make Believe
1958	30	Cozy Cole	Topsy Part 2
1955	11	Crazy Otto	Crazy Otto Medley I and II
1959	22	Dave "Baby" Cortez	The Happy Organ
1958	4	David Seville	Witch Doctor
1954	16	Dean Martin	That's Amore
1956	9	Dean Martin	Memories Are Made Of This

1958	10	Dean Martin	Return to Me
1956	60	Dick Hyman	Moritat (Theme From Threepenny Opera)
1958	1	Domenico Modugno	Volare
1956	38	Don Cherry	Band Of Gold
1952	26	Don Cornell	I'm Yours
1952	27	Don Cornell	I'll Walk Alone
1954	23	Don Cornell	Hold My Hand
1958	51	Don Gibson	Oh Lonesome Me
1956	43	Don Robertson	The Happy Whistler
1956	85	Don Rondo	Two Different Worlds
1957	69	Don Rondo	White Silver Sands
1958	46	Duane Eddy	Rebel-'Rouser
1959	58	Duane Eddy	Forty Miles Of Bad Road
1958	58	Earl Grant	The End
1958	77	Ed Townsend	For Your Love
1958	74	Eddie Cochran	Summertime Blues
1953	4	Eddie Fisher	I'm Walking Behind You
1953	28	Eddie Fisher	With These Hands
1954	6	Eddie Fisher	Oh! My Pa-pa
1954	13	Eddie Fisher	I Need You Now
1956	56	Eddie Fisher	Dungaree Doll
1956	58	Eddie Fisher	Cindy Oh Cindy
1956	54	Eddy Heywood	Soft Summer Breeze
1951	16	Eddy Howard	(It's No) Sin
1956	1	Elvis Presley	Heartbreak Hotel
1956	2	Elvis Presley	Don't Be Cruel
1956	8	Elvis Presley	Hound Dog
1956	14	Elvis Presley	I Want You, I Need You, I Love You

1956	15	Elvis Presley	Love Me Tender
1957	1	Elvis Presley	All Shook Up
1957	9	Elvis Presley	Too Much
1957	14	Elvis Presley	Teddy Bear
1957	16	Elvis Presley	Jailhouse Rock
1957	56	Elvis Presley	Love Me Tender
1957	98	Elvis Presley	Loving You
1958	3	Elvis Presley	Don't
1958	22	Elvis Presley	Wear My Ring Around Your Neck
1958	49	Elvis Presley	Hard Headed Woman
1958	55	Elvis Presley	One Night
1958	65	Elvis Presley	I Got Stung
1959	30	Elvis Presley	A Big Hunk O' Love
1959	34	Elvis Presley	(Now And Then There's) A Fool Such As I
1959	44	Elvis Presley	I Need Your Love Tonight
1959	93	Elvis Presley	My Wish Came True
1957	86	Ernie Freeman	Raunchy
1959	41	Fabian	Tiger
1959	55	Fabian	Turn Me Loose
1956	25	Fats Domino	I'm In Love Again
1956	41	Fats Domino	Blueberry Hill
1956	92	Fats Domino	My Blue Heaven
1957	38	Fats Domino	I'm Walkin'
1957	48	Fats Domino	Blueberry Hill
1957	50	Fats Domino	Blue Monday
1957	87	Fats Domino	Valley of Tears
1959	68	Fats Domino	I Want To Walk You Home
1957	23	Ferlin Husky	Gone

1955	22	Fess Parker	The Ballad Of Davy Crockett
1959	52	Franck Pourcel	Only You
1953	12	Frank Chacksfield	Ebb Tide
1953	27	Frank Chacksfield	Limelight (Terry's Theme)
1954	11	Frank Sinatra	Young At Heart
1955	14	Frank Sinatra	Learnin' The Blues
1956	53	Frank Sinatra	Hey Jealous Lover
1958	54	Frank Sinatra	All the Way
1954	17	Frank Weir	The Happy Wanderer
1958	86	Frankie Avalon	DeDe Dinah
1958	99	Frankie Avalon	I'll Wait for You
1958	100	Frankie Avalon	Ginger Bread
1959	4	Frankie Avalon	Venus
1959	59	Frankie Avalon	Just Ask Your Heart
1959	70	Frankie Avalon	Bobby Sox To Stockings
1959	82	Frankie Avalon	A Boy Without A Girl
1959	89	Frankie Ford	Sea Cruise
1950	30	Frankie Laine	Cry Of The Wild Goose
1951	11	Frankie Laine	Jezebel
1951	23	Frankie Laine	Rose, Rose I Love You
1952	19	Frankie Laine	High Noon
1953	10	Frankie Laine	I Believe
1957	32	Frankie Laine	Moonlight Gambler
1959	40	Freddie Cannon	Tallahassee Lassie
1956	27	Gene Vincent	Be-Bop-A-Lula
1957	85	Gene Vincent	Lotta Lovin'
1956	31	George Cates	Moonglow And Theme From Picnic
1956	57	George Hamilton Iv	A Rose and a Baby Ruth

1958	85	George Hamilton IV	Why Don't They Understand
1950	22	Gordon Jenkins	My Foolish Heart
1950	26	Gordon Jenkins	Bewitched
1950	7	Guy Lombardo	Third Man Theme
1956	40	Guy Mitchell	Singing The Blues
1957	7	Guy Mitchell	Singing The Blues
1957	89	Guy Mitchell	Rock-a-Billy
1959	88	Guy Mitchell	Heartaches By The Number
1957	15	Harry Belafonte	Banana Boat (Day-O)
1957	57	Harry Belafonte	Jamaica Farewell
1957	92	Harry Belafonte	Mama Look at Bubu
1959	94	Ivo Robic	Morgen
1957	62	Ivory Joe Hunter	Since I Met You Baby
1958	40	Jack Scott	My True Love
1959	79	Jack Scott	Goodbye Baby
1959	56	Jackie Wilson	Lonely Teardrops
1959	90	Jackie Wilson	That's Why
1957	28	Jerry Lee Lewis	Whole Lotta Shakin' Goin' On
1958	36	Jerry Lee Lewis	Great Balls of Fire
1958	95	Jerry Lee Lewis	Breathless
1957	64	Jerry Lewis	Rock-a-Bye Your Baby with a Dixie Melody
1956	59	Jerry Vale	You Don't Know Me
1959	47	Jerry Wallace	Primrose Lane
1956	19	Jim Lowe	The Green Door
1957	44	Jim Lowe	The Green Door
1957	63	Jim Reeves	Four Walls
1957	27	Jimmie Rodgers	Honeycomb

1958	19	Jimmie Rodgers	Secretly
1958	59	Jimmie Rodgers	Kisses Sweeter Than Wine
1957	99	Jimmy Bowen	I'm Sticking with You
1958	25	Jimmy Clanton	Just a Dream
1957	5	Jimmy Dorsey	So Rare
1958	83	Jimmy McCracklin	The Walk
1958	41	Jody Reynolds	Endless Sleep
1956	62	Joe Valino	Garden of Eden
1952	3	Johnnie Ray	Cry
1952	18	Johnnie Ray	The Little White Cloud That Cried
1952	24	Johnnie Ray	Walkin' My Baby Back Home
1952	30	Johnnie Ray	Please, Mr. Sun
1956	23	Johnnie Ray	Just Walking In The Rain
1956	81	Johnny Cash	I Walk the Line
1958	81	Johnny Cash	Ballad of a Teenage Queen
1958	91	Johnny Cash	Guess Things Happen That Way
1959	1	Johnny Horton	The Battle Of New Orleans
1957	34	Johnny Mathis	It's Not For Me To Say
1957	39	Johnny Mathis	Chances Are
1957	51	Johnny Mathis	Wonderful! Wonderful!
1958	69	Johnny Otis Show	Willie and the Hand Jive
1952	22	Johnny Standley	It's In The Book
1953	18	Julius La Rosa	Eh Cumpari
1957	43	Larry Williams	Short Fat Fanny
1957	91	Larry Williams	Bony Maronie
1956	96	Lawrence Welk	Tonight You Belong to Me
1952	1	Leroy Anderson	Blue Tango

1951	30	Les Baxter	Because Of You
1953	7	Les Baxter	April In Portugal
1955	5	Les Baxter	Unchained Melody
1956	6	Les Baxter	The Poor People Of Paris
1952	25	Les Paul	Meet Mr. Callaghan
1956	45	Little Richard	Long Tall Sally
1957	80	Little Richard	Jenny Jenny
1957	82	Little Richard	Keep a Knockin'
1959	3	Lloyd Price	Personality
1959	13	Lloyd Price	Stagger Lee
1959	23	Lloyd Price	I'm Gonna Get Married
1956	50	Lonnie Donegan	Rock Island Line
1958	80	Lou Monte	Lazy Mary
1957	65	Mantovani	Around the World
1951	5	Mario Lanza	Be My Love
1951	9	Mario Lanza	Loveliest Night Of The Year
1959	18	Martin Denny	Quiet Village
1957	17	Marty Robbins	A White Sport Coat (And A Pink Carnation)
1958	98	Marty Robbins	The Story of My Life
1957	95	Marvin Rainwater	Gonna Find Me a Bluebird
1955	3	Mitch Miller	The Yellow Rose Of Texas
1956	66	Mitch Miller	Song For a Summer Night
1958	61	Mitch Miller	March From the River Kwai and Colonel Bogey March
1956	11	Morris Stoloff	Moonglow And Theme From "Picnic"
1950	2	Nat King Cole	Mona Lisa
1951	1	Nat King Cole	Too Young
1953	13	Nat King Cole	Pretend

1954	18	Nat King Cole	Answer Me My Love
1955	20	Nat King Cole	A Blossom Fell
1956	72	Nat King Cole	That's All There Is to That
1956	88	Nat King Cole	Night Lights
1957	40	Nat King Cole	Send For Me
1958	31	Nat King Cole	Looking Back
1956	3	Nelson Riddle	Lisbon Antigua
1956	47	Nervous Norvus	Transfusion
1955	9	Pat Boone	Ain't That A Shame
1956	13	Pat Boone	I Almost Lost My Mind
1956	34	Pat Boone	I'll Be Home
1956	52	Pat Boone	Friendly Persuasion (Thee I Love)
1956	83	Pat Boone	Tutti-Frutti
1957	2	Pat Boone	Love Letters In The Sand
1957	6	Pat Boone	Don't Forbid Me
1957	58	Pat Boone	Why Baby Why
1957	81	Pat Boone	Bernardine
1957	88	Pat Boone	Remember You're Mine
1958	24	Pat Boone	A Wonderful Time Up There
1958	45	Pat Boone	April Love
1958	82	Pat Boone	It's Too Soon to Know
1958	87	Pat Boone	Sugar Moon
1957	24	Paul Anka	Diana
1958	78	Paul Anka	You Are My Destiny
1959	5	Paul Anka	Lonely Boy
1959	12	Paul Anka	Put Your Head On My Shoulder
1953	11	Pee Wee Hunt	Oh

1952	23	Pee Wee King	Slow Poke
1952	10	Percy Faith	Delicado
1953	1	Percy Faith	Song From Moulin Rouge
1955	1	Perez Prado	Cherry Pink And Apple Blossom White
1958	5	Perez Prado	Patricia
1950	25	Perry Como	Hoop-Dee-Doo
1951	8	Perry Como	If
1953	8	Perry Como	No Other Love
1953	9	Perry Como	Don't Let The Stars Get In Your Eyes
1953	21	Perry Como	Say You're Mine Again
1954	2	Perry Como	Wanted
1954	25	Perry Como	Papa Loves Mambo
1955	25	Perry Como	Ko Ko Mo
1956	16	Perry Como	Hot Diggity
1956	39	Perry Como	More
1956	76	Perry Como	Juke Box Baby
1956	80	Perry Como	Glendora
1957	10	Perry Como	Round And Round
1958	7	Perry Como	Catch a Falling Star
1958	84	Perry Como	Kewpie Doll
1950	15	Phil Harris	The Thing
1951	29	Phil Harris	The Thing
1959	96	Preston Epps	Bongo Rock
1954	22	Ralph Marterie	Skokiaan
1953	22	Ray Anthony	Dragnet
1959	66	Ray Anthony	Peter Gunn Theme
1959	50	Ray Charles	What'd I Say

1950	8	Red Foley	Chattanoogie Shoe Shine Boy
1953	14	Richard Hayman	Ruby
1956	98	Richard Maltby	Theme From 'the Man with the Golden Arm
1958	53	Rick Nelson	Lonesome Town
1957	25	Ricky Nelson	A Teenager's Romance
1957	42	Ricky Nelson	Be-bop Baby
1958	16	Ricky Nelson	Stood Up
1958	23	Ricky Nelson	Poor Little Fool
1958	67	Ricky Nelson	I Got a Feeling
1959	42	Ricky Nelson	Never Be Anyone Else But You
1959	74	Ricky Nelson	It's Late
1959	78	Ricky Nelson	Just A Little Too Much
1959	83	Ricky Nelson	Sweeter Than You
1959	14	Ritchie Valens	Donna
1958	56	Robin Luke	Susie Darlin'
1955	4	Roger Williams	Autumn Leaves
1958	75	Roger Williams	Near You
1958	93	Roy Hamilton	Don't Let Go
1957	41	Russ Hamilton	Rainbow
1956	77	Rusty Draper	Are You Satisfied
1957	97	Rusty Draper	Freight Train
1957	83	Sal Mineo	Start Movin'
1957	20	Sam Cooke	You Send Me
1950	9	Sammy Kaye	Harbor Lights
1959	33	Sammy Turner	Lavender Blue (Dilly Dilly)
1959	36	Sandy Nelson	Teen Beat
1956	42	Sanford Clark	The Fool

1958	12	Sheb Wooley	The Purple People Eater
1957	8	Sonny James	Young Love
1953	15	Stan Freberg	St. George And The Dragonet
1957	73	Steve Lawrence	Party Doll
1959	32	Stonewall Jackson	Waterloo
1957	4	Tab Hunter	Young Love
1955	13	Tennessee Ernie Ford	Sixteen Tons
1955	24	Tennessee Ernie Ford	The Ballad Of Davy Crockett
1956	22	Tennessee Ernie Ford	Sixteen Tons
1957	37	Terry Gilkyson	Marianne
1958	52	The Big Bopper	Chantilly Lace
1959	38	Thomas Wayne	Tragedy
1957	72	Thurston Harris	Little Bitty Pretty One
1958	9	Tommy Edwards	It's All in the Game
1957	33	Tommy Sands	Teenage Crush
1951	2	Tony Bennett	Because Of You
1951	7	Tony Bennett	Cold, Cold Heart
1953	19	Tony Bennett	Rags To Riches
1954	19	Tony Bennett	Stranger In Paradise
1954	27	Tony Bennett	Rags To Riches
1956	82	Tony Bennett	Can You Find It in Your Heart
1957	66	Tony Bennett	In the Middle of an Island
1950	14	Tony Martin	There's No Tomorrow
1951	12	Tony Martin	I Get Ideas
1954	30	Tony Martin	Here
1956	74	Tony Martin	Walk Hand in Hand
1951	17	Vaughn Monroe	Sound Off
1956	35	Vic Damone	On The Street Where You Live

Greatest Hits of the 1950s

1957	75	Victor Young	Around the World
1959	9	Wilbert Harrison	Kansas City
1958	64	Will Glahe	Liechtensteiner Polka
1959	71	Wink Martindale	Deck Of Cards

THE WOMEN

Women make up the smallest portion of the Top 100 with only 83 of the 580 positions (14.3%). However, 41 different women appear on the list. The top three women (Patti Page, Rosemary Clooney and Teresa Brewer) account for 22 hits, with Patti Page being the only woman to crack into the top 5 list of repeat performers at number 4 (behind Elvis Presley, Perry Como and Pat Boone).

Like with the men, numerous women also appeared as members of groups or duets and those appearances on the Master List do not appear in this chart.

Year	#	Artist	Song Title
1959	76	Annette Funicello	Tall Paul
1957	59	Betty Johnson	I Dreamed
1957	77	Bonnie Guitar	Dark Moon
1956	32	Cathy Carr	Ivory Tower
1958	39	Connie Francis	Who's Sorry Now?
1959	28	Connie Francis	Lipstick On Your Collar
1959	39	Connie Francis	My Happiness
1959	61	Connie Francis	Frankie
1951	24	Del Wood	Down Yonder
1959	43	Della Reese	Don't You Know
1951	18	Dinah Shore	Sweet Violets

1959	45	Dinah Washington	What A Diff'rence A Day Makes
1959	15	Dodie Stevens	Pink Shoelaces
1952	17	Doris Day	A Guy Is A Guy
1954	9	Doris Day	Secret Love
1954	20	Doris Day	If I Give My Heart To You
1956	7	Doris Day	Whatever Will Be Will Be (Que Sera Sera)
1953	29	Eartha Kitt	C'est Si Bon
1950	11	Eileen Barton	If I Knew You Were Coming I'd've Baked A Cake
1956	94	Eileen Rodgers	Miracle of Love
1952	14	Ella Mae Morse	Blacksmith Blues
1956	61	Gale Storm	Ivory Tower
1956	67	Gale Storm	Why Do Fools Fall in Love
1956	68	Gale Storm	Teen Age Prayer
1957	29	Gale Storm	Dark Moon
1952	11	Georgia Gibbs	Kiss Of Fire
1955	10	Georgia Gibbs	Dance With Me Henry
1955	16	Georgia Gibbs	Tweedle Dee
1955	26	Gisele Mackenzie	Hard To Get
1956	5	Gogi Grant	The Wayward Wind
1956	86	Jane Powell	True Love
1955	28	Jaye P. Morgan	That's All I Want From You
1952	4	Jo Stafford	You Belong To Me
1952	15	Jo Stafford	Jambalaya
1954	5	Jo Stafford	Make Love To Me
1956	78	Jo Stafford	It's Almost Tomorrow
1955	19	Joan Weber	Let Me Go Lover
1958	41	Jody Reynolds	Endless Sleep

1953	26	Joni James	Your Cheating Heart
1953	30	Joni James	Have You Heard?
1953	24	June Valli	Crying In The Chapel
1958	90	Kathy Linden	Billy
1959	85	Kathy Linden	Goodbye, Jimmy, Goodbye
1950	12	Kay Starr	Bonaparte's Retreat
1952	2	Kay Starr	Wheel Of Fortune
1954	21	Kay Starr	If You Love Me (Really Love Me)
1956	10	Kay Starr	Rock And Roll Waltz
1956	73	Kit Carson	Band of Gold
1954	1	Kitty Kallen	Little Things Mean A Lot
1954	28	Kitty Kallen	In The Chapel In The Moonlight
1958	17	Laurie London	He's Got the Whole World in His Hands
1957	94	Lavern Baker	Jim Dandy
1959	63	Lavern Baker	I Cried A Tear
1957	90	Margie Rayburn	I'm Available
1950	18	Patti Page	Tennessee Waltz
1950	21	Patti Page	All My Love
1951	10	Patti Page	Tennessee Waltz
1951	14	Patti Page	Mockin' Bird Hill
1951	26	Patti Page	Would I Love You
1952	8	Patti Page	I Went To Your Wedding
1953	3	Patti Page	Doggie In The Window
1954	14	Patti Page	Cross Over The Bridge
1954	24	Patti Page	Changing Partners
1956	24	Patti Page	Allegheny Moon
1956	71	Patti Page	Mama From the Train

1957	46	Patti Page	Old Cape Cod
1956	91	Peggy Lee	Mr. Wonderful
1958	76	Peggy Lee	Fever
1958	56	Robin Luke	Susie Darlin'
1951	4	Rosemary Clooney	Come On-a My House
1952	6	Rosemary Clooney	Half As Much
1952	16	Rosemary Clooney	Botch-a-me
1954	3	Rosemary Clooney	Hey There
1954	12	Rosemary Clooney	This Ole House
1959	36	Sandy Nelson	Teen Beat
1959	51	Sarah Vaughan	Broken-hearted Melody
1953	20	Silvana Mangano	Anna
1950	6	Teresa Brewer	Music, Music, Music
1953	6	Teresa Brewer	Till I Waltz Again With You
1956	46	Teresa Brewer	Sweet Old Fashioned Girl
1956	49	Teresa Brewer	A Tear Fell
1956	99	Teresa Brewer	Bo Weevil
1952	5	Vera Lynn	Auf Wiederseh'n, Sweetheart

THE GROUPS/ DUOS

Groups (including duos) double the amount of appearances on the charts as women but only half as much as the men. Groups account for 165 songs (28.4%). It is difficult to state how many groups appeared due to the duets. Many singers switched partners in duets, groups performed with others artists, and some group members might be named separately from the group (such as Buddy Holly and The Crickets having one listing and The Crickets having two others). This skews the numbers somewhat; however, essentially 100 Groups/duos appear in the list.

Year	#	Artist	Song Title
1950	16	Ames Brothers	Sentimental Me
1950	23	Ames Brothers	Rag Mop
1950	27	Ames Brothers	Can Anyone Explain?
1953	5	Ames Brothers	You, You, You
1955	27	Ames Brothers	The Naughty Lady Of Shady Lane
1956	48	Ames Brothers	It Only Hurts For A Little While
1957	71	Ames Brothers	Melodie D'Amour
1951	28	Ames Brothers and Les Brown	Undecided
1950	17	Andrews Sisters and Gordon Jenkins	I Wanna Be Loved

1950	19	Andrews Sisters and Gordon Jenkins	I Can Dream, Can't I
1958	79	Art and Dotty Todd	Chanson D'Amour
1954	26	Bill Haley and His Comets	Shake, Rattle And Roll
1955	2	Bill Haley and His Comets	Rock Around The Clock
1956	33	Bill Haley and His Comets	See You Later Alligator
1957	54	Billy Ward and His Dominoes	Star Dust
1956	44	Bing Crosby and Grace Kelly	True Love
1956	100	Blue Stars	Lullaby of Birdland
1957	47	Bobbettes	Mr. Lee
1959	7	Browns	The Three Bells
1956	30	Buchanan and Goodman	The Flying Saucer
1958	50	Buddy Holly & The Crickets	Peggy Sue
1959	75	Chris Barber's Jazz Band	Petite Fleur
1958	20	Danny & the Juniors	At the Hop
1959	48	David Seville and The Chipmunks	Alvin's Harmonica
1959	67	David Seville and The Chipmunks	The Chipmunk Song
1951	22	Debbie Reynolds and Carleton Carpenter	Aba Daba Honeymoon
1957	18	Del-Vikings	Come Go With Me
1957	49	Del-Vikings	Whispering Bells
1959	25	Dion and The Belmonts	A Teenager In Love
1956	51	Dream Weavers	It's Almost Tomorrow
1952	7	Eddie Fisher and Hugo Winterhalter	Wish You Were Here
1952	12	Eddie Fisher and Hugo Winterhalter	Anytime

1952	20	Eddie Fisher and Hugo Winterhalter	I'm Yours
1952	28	Eddie Fisher and Hugo Winterhalter	Tell Me Why
1956	17	Eddie Heywood and Hugo Winterhalter	Canadian Sunset
1959	37	Edward Burns and Connie Stevens	Kookie Kookie (Lend Me Your Comb)
1959	99	Ernie Fields Orchestra	In The Mood
1959	69	Fiestas	So Fine
1959	8	Fleetwoods	Come Softly To Me
1959	10	Fleetwoods	Mr. Blue
1955	15	Fontaine Sisters	Hearts Of Stone
1956	84	Fontane Sisters	Eddie My Love
1952	13	Four Aces	Tell Me Why
1954	8	Four Aces	Three Coins In The Fountain
1954	29	Four Aces	Stranger In Paradise
1955	7	Four Aces	Love Is A Many Splendored Thing
1951	21	Four Aces and Al Alberts	(It's No) Sin
1957	96	Four Coins	Shangri-La
1954	7	Four Knights	I Get So Lonely
1955	17	Four Lads	Moments To Remember
1956	20	Four Lads	No, Not Much
1956	29	Four Lads	Standing On The Corner
1957	70	Four Lads	Who Needs You
1958	57	Four Preps	26 Miles
1958	70	Four Preps	Big Man
1953	23	Frankie Laine and Jimmy Boyd	Tell Me A Story

1956	28	Frankie Lymon and The Teenagers	Why Do Fools Fall In Love
1956	95	Frankie Lymon and the Teenagers	I Want You to Be My Girl
1950	4	Gary and Bing Crosby	Sam's Song
1950	5	Gary and Bing Crosby	Simple Melody
1953	17	Gaylords	Tell Me You're Mine
1954	15	Gaylords	The Little Shoemaker
1950	1	Gordon Jenkins and The Weavers	Goodnight Irene
1950	13	Gordon Jenkins and The Weavers	Tzena, Tzena, Tzena
1951	15	Guy Mitchell and Mitch Miller	My Heart Cries For You
1951	20	Guy Mitchell and Mitch Miller	My Truly, Truly Fair
1952	29	Hilltoppers	Trying
1953	16	Hilltoppers	P.S. I Love You
1957	68	Hilltoppers	Marianne
1958	94	Hollywood Flames	Buzz-Buzz-Buzz
1959	24	Impalas	Sorry (I Ran All The Way Home)
1958	96	Jan and Arnie	Jennie Lee
1959	95	Jan and Dean	Baby Talk
1957	52	Jane Morgan and the Troubadours	Fascination
1957	100	Joe Bennett and the Sparkletones	Black Slacks
1957	67	Johnnie and Joe	Over the Mountain Across the Sea

1959	31	Johnny and The Hurricanes	Red River Rock
1951	3	Les Paul and Mary Ford	How High The Moon
1951	13	Les Paul and Mary Ford	Mockin' Bird Hill
1951	19	Les Paul and Mary Ford	The World Is Waiting For The Sunrise
1953	2	Les Paul and Mary Ford	Vaya Con Dios
1958	34	Little Anthony and the Imperials	Tears on My Pillow
1957	78	Mickey and Sylvia	Love Is Strange
1959	98	Mormon Tabernacle Choir	Battle Hymn Of The Republic
1956	64	Otis Williams and the Charms	Ivory Tower
1956	26	Patience and Prudence	Tonight You Belong To Me
1957	93	Patience and Prudence	Gonna Get Along Without Ya Now
1959	100	Paul Evans and The Curls	(Seven Little Girls) Sitting In The Back Seat
1951	27	Perry Como and The Fontane Sisters	You're Just In Love
1959	21	Phil Phillips and The Twilights	Sea Of Love
1957	35	Rays	Silhouettes
1959	86	Reg Owens Orch.	Manhattan Spiritual
1956	87	Richard Hayman and Jan August	Moritat
1958	35	Royal Teens	Short Shorts
1950	10	Sammy Kaye and Don Cornell	It Isn't Fair
1959	11	Santo and Johnny	Sleep Walk

1959	84	Skip and Flip	It Was I
1959	65	Skyliners	Since I Don't Have You
1955	30	Somethin' Smith and The Redheads	It's A Sin To Tell A Lie
1957	26	Tarriers	The Banana Boat Song
1950	20	Tennessee Ernie Ford and Kay Starr	I'll Never Be Free
1959	62	The Bell Notes	I've Had It
1956	89	The Cadillacs	Speedoo
1958	8	The Champs	Tequila
1958	89	The Chantels	Maybe
1955	18	The Chordettes	Mr. Sandman
1956	37	The Chordettes	Born To Be With You
1956	97	The Chordettes	Lay Down Your Arms
1958	37	The Chordettes	Lollipop
1957	21	The Coasters	Searchin'
1957	74	The Coasters	Young Blood
1959	54	The Coasters	Poison Ivy
1959	80	The Coasters	Along Came Jones
1958	21	The Coasters	Yakety Yak
1959	17	The Coasters	Charlie Brown
1958	47	The Crescendos	Oh, Julie
1959	26	The Crests	16 Candles
1954	4	The Crew Cuts	Sh-Boom
1956	65	The Crew Cuts	Angels in the Sky
1957	30	The Crickets	That'll Be The Day
1958	71	The Crickets	Oh Boy
1956	75	The Diamonds	Why Do Fools Fall in Love
1956	90	The Diamonds	The Church Bells May Ring
1957	3	The Diamonds	Little Darlin'

1958	48	The Diamonds	The Stroll
1959	29	The Drifters	There Goes My Baby
1958	15	The Elegants	Little Star
1957	11	The Everly Brothers	Bye Bye Love
1957	19	The Everly Brothers	Wake Up Little Susie
1958	62	The Everly Brothers	Problems
1958	88	The Everly Brothers	Devoted to You
1959	20	The Everly Brothers	('Til) I Kissed You
1959	97	The Everly Brothers	Take A Message To Mary
1958	2	The Everly Brothers	All I Have to Do Is Dream
1958	13	The Everly Brothers	Bird Dog
1959	73	The Flamingos	I Only Have Eyes For You
1958	43	The Kalin Twins	When
1959	77	The Kingston Trio	The Tijuana Jail
1958	28	The Kingston Trio	Tom Dooley
1955	8	The McGuire Sisters	Sincerely
1956	69	The McGuire Sisters	Picnic
1958	26	The McGuire Sisters	Sugartime
1952	21	The Mills Brothers	Glow Worm
1958	32	The Monotones	The Book of Love
1958	92	The Olympics	Western Movies
1955	29	The Platters	Only You
1956	4	The Platters	My Prayer
1956	12	The Platters	The Great Pretender
1956	36	The Platters	Magic Touch
1956	79	The Platters	You'll Never Never Know
1959	16	The Platters	Smoke Gets In Your Eyes
1959	64	The Platters	Enchanted
1958	18	The Platters	Twilight Time
1958	60	The Playmates	Beep Beep

1958	68	The Poni-Tails	Born Too Late
1958	97	The Royaltones	Poor Boy
1958	14	The Silhouettes	Get a Job
1958	44	The Teddy Bears	To Know Him Is to Love Him
1959	35	The Virtues	Guitar Boogie Shuffle
1959	81	Tommy Dee and Carol Kay	Three Stars
1958	33	Tommy Dorsey Orchestra & Warren Covington	Tea For Two Cha-Cha
1959	60	Travis and Bob	Tell Him No
1957	61	Tune Weavers	Happy, Happy Birthday Baby
1956	63	Vince Martin and the Tarriers	Cindy Oh Cindy
1951	6	Weavers	On Top Of Old Smoky

ONE HIT WONDERS

This title is really a misnomer for several reasons. First, this list is only based on the annual charts. There are also weekly charts that will have successful songs that don't make the Top 100. In addition, this list is limited to the period from 1950-1959. Many of the artists had hits in the 1940's and 1960's. Therefore rather than think of these artists as necessarily one hit wonders, the proper category would be single annual hits in the 1950's. But that title isn't as glamorous.

Of the 580 songs that make up the Master List, 198 of the artists appear a single time (34.1%). However, in some cases, these artists appear as part of a duo where their partner has appeared elsewhere on the chart. In those cases, I have put the one hit wonder's name in bold.

Year	#	Artist	Song Title
1952	9	Al Martino	Here In My Heart
1959	76	Annette Funicello	Tall Paul
1950	3	Anton Karas	Third Man Theme
1954	10	Archie Bleyer	Hernando's Hideaway
1958	79	Art and Dotty Todd	Chanson D'Amour
1955	23	Art Mooney	Honey Babe
1959	62	Bell Notes	I've Had It
1957	59	Betty Johnson	I Dreamed

1956	21	Bill Doggett	Honky Tonk
1955	6	Bill Hayes	The Ballad Of Davy Crockett
1957	55	Bill Justis	Raunchy
1959	46	Bill Parsons	The All American Boy
1950	24	Bill Snyder	Bewitched
1959	53	Billy Grammer	Gotta Travel On
1957	54	Billy Ward and His Dominoes	Star Dust
1957	45	Billy Williams	I'm Gonna Sit RIght Down And Write Myself A Letter
1956	44	Bing Crosby and **Grace Kelly**	True Love
1956	100	Blue Stars	Lullaby of Birdland
1957	47	Bobbettes	Mr. Lee
1958	27	Bobby Day	Rockin' Robin
1958	42	Bobby Freeman	Do You Want to Dance
1957	53	Bobby Helms	My Special Angel
1959	92	Bobby Rydell	Kissin' Time
1957	77	Bonnie Guitar	Dark Moon
1959	7	Browns	The Three Bells
1956	30	Buchanan and Goodman	The Flying Saucer
1959	19	Carl Dobkins Jr.	My Heart Is An Open Book
1956	18	Carl Perkins	Blue Suede Shoes
1956	32	Cathy Carr	Ivory Tower
1958	89	Chantels	Maybe
1957	31	Charlie Gracie	Butterfly
1959	75	Chris Barber's Jazz Band	Petite Fleur
1958	11	Conway Twitty	It's Only Make Believe
1958	30	Cozy Cole	Topsy Part 2
1955	11	Crazy Otto	Crazy Otto Medley I and II
1959	26	Crests	16 Candles

1958	20	Danny & the Juniors	At the Hop
1959	22	Dave "Baby" Cortez	The Happy Organ
1951	22	Debbie Reynolds and **Carleton Carpenter**	Aba Daba Honeymoon
1951	24	Del Wood	Down Yonder
1959	43	Della Reese	Don't You Know
1956	60	Dick Hyman	Moritat (Theme From Threepenny Opera)
1951	18	Dinah Shore	Sweet Violets
1959	45	Dinah Washington	What A Diff'rence A Day Makes
1959	25	Dion and The Belmonts	A Teenager In Love
1959	15	Dodie Stevens	Pink Shoelaces
1958	1	Domenico Modugno	Volare
1956	38	Don Cherry	Band Of Gold
1958	51	Don Gibson	Oh Lonesome Me
1956	43	Don Robertson	The Happy Whistler
1956	51	Dream Weavers	It's Almost Tomorrow
1958	58	Earl Grant	The End
1953	29	Eartha Kitt	C'est Si Bon
1958	77	Ed Townsend	For Your Love
1958	74	Eddie Cochran	Summertime Blues
1951	16	Eddy Howard	(It's No) Sin
1959	37	Edward Burns and Connie Stevens	Kookie Kookie (Lend Me Your Comb)
1950	11	Eileen Barton	If I Knew You Were Coming I'd've Baked A Cake
1956	94	Eileen Rodgers	Miracle of Love
1952	14	Ella Mae Morse	Blacksmith Blues
1959	99	Ernie Fields Orchestra	In The Mood

1957	86	Ernie Freeman	Raunchy
1959	91	Falcons	You're So Fine
1957	23	Ferlin Husky	Gone
1955	22	Fess Parker	The Ballad Of Davy Crockett
1959	69	Fiestas	So Fine
1959	73	Flamingos	I Only Have Eyes For You
1957	96	Four Coins	Shangri-La
1954	7	Four Knights	I Get So Lonely
1959	52	Franck Pourcel	Only You
1954	17	Frank Weir	The Happy Wanderer
1959	89	Frankie Ford	Sea Cruise
1953	23	Frankie Laine and **Jimmy Boyd**	Tell Me A Story
1959	40	Freddie Cannon	Tallahassee Lassie
1956	31	George Cates	Moonglow And Theme From Picnic
1955	26	Gisele Mackenzie	Hard To Get
1956	5	Gogi Grant	The Wayward Wind
1950	7	Guy Lombardo	Third Man Theme
1958	94	Hollywood Flames	Buzz-Buzz-Buzz
1959	24	Impalas	Sorry (I Ran All The Way Home)
1959	94	Ivo Robic	Morgen
1957	62	Ivory Joe Hunter	Since I Met You Baby
1958	96	Jan and **Arnie**	Jennie Lee
1959	95	Jan and **Dean**	Baby Talk
1957	52	Jane Morgan and the Troubadours	Fascination
1956	86	Jane Powell	True Love
1955	28	Jaye P. Morgan	That's All I Want From You

1957	64	Jerry Lewis	Rock-a-Bye Your Baby with a Dixie Melody
1956	59	Jerry Vale	You Don't Know Me
1959	47	Jerry Wallace	Primrose Lane
1957	63	Jim Reeves	Four Walls
1957	99	Jimmy Bowen	I'm Sticking with You
1958	25	Jimmy Clanton	Just a Dream
1957	5	Jimmy Dorsey	So Rare
1958	83	Jimmy McCracklin	The Walk
1955	19	Joan Weber	Let Me Go Lover
1958	41	Jody Reynolds	Endless Sleep
1957	100	Joe Bennett and the Sparkletones	Black Slacks
1956	62	Joe Valino	Garden of Eden
1957	67	Johnnie and Joe	Over the Mountain Across the Sea
1959	31	Johnny and The Hurricanes	Red River Rock
1959	1	Johnny Horton	The Battle Of New Orleans
1958	69	Johnny Otis Show	Willie and the Hand Jive
1952	22	Johnny Standley	It's In The Book
1953	18	Julius La Rosa	Eh Cumpari
1953	24	June Valli	Crying In The Chapel
1956	73	Kit Carson	Band of Gold
1958	17	Laurie London	He's Got the Whole World in His Hands
1956	96	Lawrence Welk	Tonight You Belong to Me
1952	1	Leroy Anderson	Blue Tango
1958	34	Little Anthony and the Imperials	Tears on My Pillow
1956	50	Lonnie Donegan	Rock Island Line

1958	80	Lou Monte	Lazy Mary
1957	65	Mantovani	Around the World
1957	90	Margie Rayburn	I'm Available
1959	18	Martin Denny	Quiet Village
1957	95	Marvin Rainwater	Gonna Find Me a Bluebird
1957	78	Mickey and Sylvia	Love Is Strange
1952	21	Mills Brothers	Glow Worm
1959	98	Mormon Tabernacle Choir	Battle Hymn Of The Republic
1956	11	Morris Stoloff	Moonglow And Theme From "Picnic"
1956	3	Nelson Riddle	Lisbon Antigua
1956	47	Nervous Norvus	Transfusion
1956	64	Otis Williams and the Charms	Ivory Tower
1959	100	Paul Evans and The Curls	(Seven Little Girls) Sitting In The Back Seat
1953	11	Pee Wee Hunt	Oh
1952	23	Pee Wee King	Slow Poke
1952	10	Percy Faith	Delicado
1953	1	Percy Faith	Song From Moulin Rouge
1951	27	Perry Como and **The Fontaine Sisters**	You're Just In Love
1950	15	Phil Harris	The Thing
1951	29	Phil Harris	The Thing
1959	21	Phil Phillips and The Twilights	Sea Of Love
1959	96	Preston Epps	Bongo Rock
1954	22	Ralph Marterie	Skokiaan
1959	50	Ray Charles	What'd I Say

1957	35	Rays	Silhouettes
1950	8	Red Foley	Chattanoogie Shoe Shine Boy
1959	86	Reg Owens Orch.	Manhattan Spiritual
1956	87	Richard Hayman and **Jan August**	Moritat
1956	98	Richard Maltby	Theme From 'the Man with the Golden Arm
1959	14	Ritchie Valens	Donna
1958	56	Robin Luke	Susie Darlin'
1958	93	Roy Hamilton	Don't Let Go
1958	35	Royal Teens	Short Shorts
1957	41	Russ Hamilton	Rainbow
1957	83	Sal Mineo	Start Movin'
1957	20	Sam Cooke	You Send Me
1959	33	Sammy Turner	Lavender Blue (Dilly Dilly)
1959	36	Sandy Nelson	Teen Beat
1956	42	Sanford Clark	The Fool
1959	11	Santo and Johnny	Sleep Walk
1959	51	Sarah Vaughan	Broken-hearted Melody
1958	12	Sheb Wooley	The Purple People Eater
1953	20	Silvana Mangano	Anna
1959	84	Skip and Flip	It Was I
1959	65	Skyliners	Since I Don't Have You
1955	30	Somethin' Smith and The Redheads	It's A Sin To Tell A Lie
1957	8	Sonny James	Young Love
1953	15	Stan Freberg	St. George And The Dragonet
1957	73	Steve Lawrence	Party Doll

1959	32	Stonewall Jackson	Waterloo
1957	4	Tab Hunter	Young Love
1957	26	Tarriers	The Banana Boat Song
1957	37	Terry Gilkyson	Marianne
1958	52	The Big Bopper	Chantilly Lace
1956	89	The Cadillacs	Speedoo
1958	8	The Champs	Tequila
1958	47	The Crescendos	Oh, Julie
1959	29	The Drifters	There Goes My Baby
1958	15	The Elegants	Little Star
1958	43	The Kalin Twins	When
1958	32	The Monotones	The Book of Love
1958	92	The Olympics	Western Movies
1958	60	The Playmates	Beep Beep
1958	68	The Poni-Tails	Born Too Late
1958	97	The Royaltones	Poor Boy
1958	14	The Silhouettes	Get a Job
1958	44	The Teddy Bears	To Know Him Is to Love Him
1959	35	The Virtues	Guitar Boogie Shuffle
1959	38	Thomas Wayne	Tragedy
1957	72	Thurston Harris	Little Bitty Pretty One
1959	81	Tommy Dee and Carol Kay	Three Stars
1958	33	Tommy Dorsey Orchestra & Warren Covington	Tea For Two Cha-Cha
1958	9	Tommy Edwards	It's All in the Game
1957	33	Tommy Sands	Teenage Crush
1959	60	Travis and Bob	Tell Him No
1957	61	Tune Weavers	Happy, Happy Birthday Baby
1951	17	Vaughn Monroe	Sound Off

1952	5	Vera Lynn	Auf Wiederseh'n, Sweetheart
1956	35	Vic Damone	On The Street Where You Live
1957	75	Victor Young	Around the World
1956	63	Vince Martin and the Tarriers	Cindy Oh Cindy
1959	9	Wilbert Harrison	Kansas City
1958	64	Will Glahe	Liechtensteiner Polka
1959	71	Wink Martindale	Deck Of Cards

REPEATERS

These are the big winners of the 1950's music industry: those artists that had more than one hit. 104 different artists came away with at least two hits. The top five artists accounted for a whopping 72 hits! Five artists accounted for 12.4% of the entire list. The top ten artists account for nearly 20% (19.4%).

The breakdown is this:

1 artist= 20 hits
1 artist= 16 hits
1 artist=14 hits
1 artist=12 hits
1 artist=10 hits
1 artist=9 hits
4 artists=8 hits
3 artists=7 hits
3 artists=6 hits
5 artists=5 hits
17 artists=4 hits
17 artists=3 hits and
48 artists=2 hits

Name	# of hits	Song Titles
Elvis Presley	20	Heartbreak Hotel; Don't Be Cruel; Hound Dog; I Want You, I Need You, I Love You; Love Me Tender (two years); All Shook Up; Too Much; Teddy Bear; Jailhouse Rock; Loving You; Don't; Wear My Ring Around Your Neck; Hard Headed Woman; One Night; I Got Stung; A Big Hunk O' Love; (Now And Then There's) A Fool Such As I; I Need Your Love Tonight; My Wish Came True
Perry Como	16	Hoop-Dee-Doo; If; No Other Love; Don't Let The Stars Get In Your Eyes; Say You're Mine Again; Wanted; Papa Loves Mambo; Ko Ko Mo; Hot Diggity; More; Juke Box Baby; Glendora; Round and Round; Catch A Falling Star; Kewpie Doll; You're Just In Love (with The Fontaine Sisters)

Pat Boone	14	Ain't That A Shame; I Almost Lost My Mind; I'll Be Home; Friendly Persuasion (Thee I Love); Tutti-Frutti; Love Letters In The Sand; Don't Forbid Me; Why Baby Why; Bernadine; Remember You're Mine; A Wonderful Time Up There; April Love; It's Too Soon To Know; Sugar Moon
Patti Page	12	Tennessee Waltz (two years); All My Love; Tennessee Waltz; Mockin' Bird Hill; Would I Love You; I Went To Your Wedding; Doggie In The Window; Cross Over The Bridge; Changing Partners; Allegheny Moon; Mama From The Train; Old Cape Cod
Ricky Nelson	10	Lonesome Town; A Teenager's Romance; Be-Bop Baby; Stood Up; Poor Little Fool; I Got A Feeling; Never Be Anyone Else But You; It's Late; Just A Little Too Much; Sweeter Than You

Nat King Cole	9	Mona Lisa; Too Young; Pretend; Answer Me My Love; A Blossom Fell; That's All There Is to That; Night Lights; Send For Me; Looking Back
Ames Brothers	8	Sentimental Me; Rag Mop; Can Anyone Explain?; You, You, You; The Naughty Lady Of Shady Lane; It Only Hurts For A Little While; Melodie D'Amour; Undecided (with Les Brown)
Fats Domino	8	I'm In Love Again; Blueberry Hill (2 years); My Blue Heaven; I'm Walkin'; Blue Monday; Valley of Tears; I Want To Walk You Home
The Everly Brothers	8	Bye Bye Love; Wake Up Little Susie; Problems; Devoted To You; ('Til) I Kissed You; Take A Message To Mary; All I Have to Do Is Dream; Bird Dog
The Platters	8	Only You; My Prayer; The Great Pretender; Magic Touch; You'll Never Never Know; Smoke Gets In Your Eyes; Enchanted; Twilight Time

Frankie Avalon	7	DeDe Dinah; I'll Wait For You; Ginger Bread; Venus; Just ask Your Heart; Bobby Sox to Stockings; A Boy Without A Girl
Frankie Laine	7	Cry Of The Wild Goose; Jezebel; Rose, Rose I Love You; High Noon; I Believe, Moonlight Gambler; Tell Me A Story (with Jimmy Boyd)
Tony Bennett	7	Because Of You; Cold, Cold Heart; Rags To Riches (two years); Stranger In Paradise; Can You Find It in Your Heart; In the Middle of an Island
Andy Williams	6	Canadian Sunset; Butterfly; I Like Your Kind Of Love; Are You Sincere; Lonely Street; Hawaiian Wedding Song
Eddie Fisher	6	I'm Walking Behind You; With These Hands; Oh! My Pa-pa; I Need You Now; Dungaree Doll; Cindy Oh Cindy
The Coasters	6	Searchin'; Young Blood; Poison Ivy; Along Came Jones; Yakity Yak; Charlie Brown

Four Aces aka Four Aces Featuring Al Alberts	5	Tell Me Why; Three Coins In The Fountain; Stranger In Paradise; Love Is A Many Splendored Thing; (It's No) Sin
Johnnie Ray	5	Cry; The Little White Cloud That Cried; Walkin' My Baby Back Home; Please, Mr. Sun; Just Walking In The Rain
Les Paul (with Mary Ford on 4)	5	Meet Mr. Callaghan; How High The Moon(with Mary Ford); Mockin' Bird Hill(with Mary Ford); The World Is Waiting For The Sunrise (with Mary Ford); Vaya Con Dios (with Mary Ford)
Rosemary Clooney	5	Come On-a My House; Half As Much; Botch-a-me; Hey There; This Ole House
Teresa Brewer	5	Music, Music, Music; Till I Waltz Again With You; Sweet Old Fashioned Girl; A Tear Fell; Bo Weevil
Bobby Darin	4	Splish Splash; Queen of the Hop; Mack the Knife; Dream Lover
Chuck Berry	4	School Day; Rock and Roll Music; Sweet Little Sixteen; Johnny B Goode

Connie Francis	4	Who's Sorry Now?; Lipstick On Your Collar; My Happiness; Frankie
Doris Day	4	A Guy Is A Guy; Secret Love; If I Give My Heart To You; Whatever Will Be Will Be (Que Sera Sera)
Eddie Fisher and Hugo Winterhalter	4	Wish You Were Here; Anytime; I'm Yours; Tell Me Why
Four Lads	4	Moments To Remember; No, Not Much; Standing On The Corner; Who Needs You
Frank Sinatra	4	Young At Heart; Learnin' The Blues; Hey Jealous Lover; All The Way
Gale Storm	4	Ivory Tower; Why Do Fools Fall in Love; Teen Age Prayer; Dark Moon
Guy Mitchell	4	Singing The Blues (two years); Rock-A-Billy; Heartaches By the Number
Jo Stafford	4	You Belong To Me; Jambalaya; Make Love To Me; It's Almost Tomorrow
Kay Starr	4	Bonaparte's Retreat; Wheel of Fortune; If You Love Me (Really Love Me); Rock And Roll Waltz

Les Baxter	4	Because Of You; Unchained Melody; The Poor People Of Paris
Paul Anka	4	Diana; You Are My Destiny; Lonely Boy; Put Your Head On My Shoulder
Tennessee Ernie Ford	4	Sixteen Tons (two years); The Ballad Of Davy Crockett; I'll Never Be Free (with Kay Starr)
The Chordettes	4	Mr. Sandman; Born To Be With You; Lay Down Your Arms; Lollipop
The Diamonds	4	Why Do Fools Fall in Love; The Church Bells May Ring; Little Darlin'; The Stroll
Tony Martin	4	There's No Tomorrow; I Get Ideas; Here; Walk Hand in Hand
Bill Haley and His Comets	3	Shake, Rattle And Roll; Rock Around The Clock; See You Later Alligator
The Crickets aka Buddy Holly & The Crickets	3	Peggy Sue; That'll Be The Day; Oh Boy
David Seville aka David Seville and The Chipmunks	3	Witch Doctor; Alvin's Harmonica (with the Chipmunks); The Chipmunk Song (with the Chipmunks)
Dean Martin	3	That's Amore; Memories Are Made Of This; Return To Me

Don Cornell	3	I'm Yours; I'll Walk Alone; Hold My Hand
Georgia Gibbs	3	Kiss Of Fire; Dance With Me Henry; Tweedle Dee
Harry Belafonte	3	Banana Boat (Day-O); Jamaica Farewell; Mama Look at Bubu
Hilltoppers	3	Trying; P.S. I Love You; Marianne
Jerry Lee Lewis	3	Whole Lotta Shakin' Goin' On; Great Balls of Fire; Breathless
Jimmie Rodgers	3	Honeycomb; Secretly; Kisses Sweeter Than Wine
Johnny Cash	3	I Walk the Line; Ballad of a Teenage Queen; Guess Things Happen That Way
Johnny Mathis	3	It's Not For Me To Say; Chances Are; Wonderful! Wonderful!
Joni James	3	Why Don't You Believe Me; Your Cheating Heart; Have You Heard?
Little Richard	3	Long Tall Sally; Jenny Jenny; Keep A Knockin'
Lloyd Price	3	Personality; Stagger Lee; I'm Gonna Get Married
McGuire Sisters	3	Sincerely; Picnic; ; Sugartime

Mitch Miller	3	The Yellow Rose Of Texas; Song For a Summer Night; March From the River Kwai and Colonel Bogey March
Al Hibbler	2	Unchained Melody; After the Lights Go Down Low
Andrews Sisters and Gordon Jenkins	2	I Wanna Be Loved; I Can Dream, Can't I
Billy Eckstine	2	My Foolish Heart; I Apologize
Billy Vaughn	2	Melody Of Love; Sail Along Silvery Moon
Bing Crosby	2	Dear Hearts And Gentle People; True Love (with Grace Kelly)
Brook Benton	2	It's Just A Matter Of Time; Endlessly
Buddy Knox	2	Party Doll; Hula Love
Chuck Willis	2	C.C. Rider; What Am I Living For
Clyde McPhatter	2	Treasure of Love, A Lover's Question
Crew Cuts	2	Sh-Boom; Angels In The Sky
Debbie Reynolds	2	Tammy; Aba Daba Honeymoon (with Carleton Carpenter)
Del-Vikings	2	Come Go With Me; Whispering Bells
Don Rondo	2	Two Different Worlds; White Silver Sands

Duane Eddy	2	Rebel-'Rouser; Forty Miles of Bad Road
Eddy Heywood	2	Soft Summer Breeze; Canadian Sunset (with Hugo Winterhalter)
Fabian	2	Tiger; Turn Me Loose
Fleetwoods	2	Come Softly To Me; Mr. Blue
Fontaine Sisters	2	Hearts Of Stone; Eddie My Love
Four Preps	2	26 Miles; Big Man
Frank Chacksfield	2	Ebb Tide; Limelight (Terry's Theme)
Frankie Lymon and The Teenagers	2	Why Do Fools Fall In Love; I Want You To Be My Girl
Gary and Bing Crosby	2	Sam's Song; Simple Melody
Gaylords	2	Tell Me You're Mine; The Little Shoemaker
Gene Vincent	2	Be-Bop-A-Lula; Lotta Lovin'
George Hamilton IV	2	A Rose and a Baby Ruth; Why Don't They Understand
Gordon Jenkins	2	My Foolish Heart; Bewitched
Gordon Jenkins and The Weavers	2	Goodnight Irene; Tzena, Tzena, Tzena
Guy Mitchell and Mitch Miller	2	My Heart Cries For You; My Truly, Truly Fair
Jack Scott	2	My True Love; Goodbye Baby
Jackie Wilson	2	Lonely Teardrops; That's Why

Jim Lowe	2	The Green Door (two years)
Kitty Kallen	2	Little Things Mean A Lot; In The Chapel In The Moonlight
Larry Williams	2	Short Fat Fanny; Bony Maronie
Lavern Baker	2	Jim Dandy; I Cried A Tear
Mario Lanza	2	Be My Love; Loveliest Night Of The Year
Marty Robbins	2	A White Sport Coat (And A Pink Carnation); The Story of My Life
Patience and Prudence	2	Tonight You Belong To Me; Gonna Get Along Without Ya Now
Peggy Lee	2	Mr. Wonderful; Fever
Percy Faith	2	Delicado; Song From Moulin Rouge
Perez Prado	2	Cherry Pink And Apple Blossom White; Patricia
Phil Harris	2	The Thing (two years)
Ray Anthony	2	Dragnet; Peter Gunn Theme
Richard Hayman	2	Ruby; Moritat (with Jan August)
Roger Williams	2	Autumn Leaves; Near You
Rusty Draper	2	Are You Satisfied; Freight Train
Sammy Kaye	2	Harbor Lights; It Isn't Fair (with Don Cornell)
The Kingston Trio	2	The Tijuana Jail; Tom Dooley

Kathy Linden	2	Goodbye, Jimmy, Goodbye; Billy

MISCELLANEOUS TRIVIA

1950: The song Goodnight Irene was a folk song of unknown origins. Lead Belly, a blues musician popularized it. In 1934 Lead Belly was in prison for attempted homicide. His request for release was presented to the Louisiana governor on the reverse side of a recording of Goodnight Irene. Lead Belly and folklorist John Lomax who delivered the request believe the song was responsible for Lead Belly's early release. A year after his death it became a #1 hit for the Weavers in 1950.

1951: Although the phrase rock and roll had been used previously in relation to R&B music, its first use to describe a genre of music was in 1951 by Cleveland DJ Alan Freed.

1952: Blue Tango by Leroy Anderson was the first instrumental recording ever to sell over one million copies.

1953: Les Paul who recorded Vaya Con Dios with Mary Ford is today better known as one of the pioneers of the solid body electric guitar and has a permanent stand-alone exhibit in the Rock and Roll Hall of Fame. He is the only person included in both the Rock and Roll Hall of Fame and the National Inventors Hall of Fame.

1954: Young At Heart by Frank Sinatra became such a huge hit that a film Sinatra was filming with Doris Day was renamed "Young At Heart" and the song was used as the title song. The song was considered Sinatra's comeback single after several years away from the charts.

1955: Rock Around The Clock by Bill Haley and His Comets was the first rock and roll song to hit the top of Billboard's Pop Chart and led the band to be the first rock and roll performers to appear on the Ed Sullivan Show.

1956: Heartbreak Hotel was Elvis Presley's first single for RCA and Elvis' first million seller. It reached Number One on both the Pop Chart and the County and Western Chart.

1957: A 1957 poll of high school students showed Pat Boone a two to one favorite over Elvis Presley among boys and nearly a three to one favorite among girls.

1958: All I Have To Do Is Dream by The Everly Brothers was the only single ever to be at the top of all of Billboard's singles Charts simultaneously (Top 100, Most Played by Jockeys, R&B, Country, Hot 100, best seller)

1959: Tom Dowd was the recording engineer for Bobby Darin's song "Mack The Knife". Dowd, whose career as an engineer lasted 55 years, is considered one of the top engineers in modern music having worked with a virtual who's who of rock, pop, soul, jazz and blues.

CLOSING

The 1950's gave us fantastic music that has withstood the test of time. Many of these songs and singers are still staples on the radio and are part of music history. The music styles showed great diversity but one thing was clear- as the decade progressed it laid the foundation and opened the door for The Greatest Hits of ... the 1960s.

Thank you for reading.
Please review this book. Reviews help others find Absolutely Amazing eBooks and inspire us to keep providing these marvelous tales.

If you would like to be put on our email list to receive updates on new releases, contests, and promotions, please go to AbsolutelyAmazingEbooks.com and sign up.

ABOUT THE AUTHOR

ALBERT L. KELLEY, is an attorney, author, book publisher, film producer, traveler and adventurer who makes his home in Key West, Florida with his wife Angie. His law practice concentrates primarily in the areas of business, corporations, contracts, copyright, trademark, and entertainment law, as well as foreclosure defense. He graduated cum laude from Florida State University College of Law in 1989. He served for years as an adjunct professor for St. Leo University in their Business Administration program, teaching courses in business, employment and administrative law. For five years Al wrote a weekly business law newspaper column and has authored a book on business law. He has also been a featured panelist at Florida State University's College of Law's Annual Entertainment Art and Sports Law Symposium. Albert L. Kelley serves as legal counsel for the world's largest offshore powerboat race promoter as well as museums, art galleries, television stations, performers and newspapers. On the business side, Albert is corporate counsel to over 150 corporations, and has filed over 60 trademark registrations and countless copyright applications. Albert has negotiated contracts with numerous national companies including Apple Computers, Harley Davidson, and Ralston Purina. Al has given numerous seminars on trademarks, copyrights, film licensing and financing, and foreclosure defenses. He is a licensed skydiver, hang-glider pilot, and scuba diver.

OTHER BOOKS BY
ALBERT L. KELLEY

Basics Of ... Business Law
Basics Of ... Florida's Small Claims Court
The Greatest Hits of ... the 1960's
The Greatest Hits of ... the 1970's
The Greatest Hits of ... the 1980's

ABSOLUTELY AMAZING eBOOKS

AbsolutelyAmazingEbooks.com
Or AA-eBooks.com

www.ingramcontent.com/pod-product-compliance
Lightning Source LLC
Chambersburg PA
CBHW070702290526
45790CB00001B/419